## POCKET GUIDE

# BIRDS
## OF BOTSWANA

DOMINIC ROLLINSON

Published by Struik Nature
(an imprint of Penguin Random House
South Africa (Pty) Ltd
Reg. No. 1953/000441/07
The Estuaries No. 4, Oxbow Crescent,
Century Avenue, Century City 7441
PO Box 1144, Cape Town 8000
South Africa

Visit **www.struiknature.co.za** and
join the Struik Nature Club for
updates, news, events and
special offers.

First published in 2025
10 9 8 7 6 5 4 3 2 1

Copyright © in text, 2025: Dominic Rollinson
Copyright © in photographs, 2025: Dominic Rollinson, unless otherwise specified
Copyright © in maps, 2025: Dominic Rollinson/Penguin Random House South Africa (Pty) Ltd
Copyright © in illustrations, 2025: Penguin Random House South Africa (Pty) Ltd
Copyright © in published edition, 2025: Penguin Random House South Africa (Pty) Ltd

**Publisher:** Pippa Parker
**Managing editor:** Roelien Theron
**Editor:** Colette Alves
**Designer:** Emily de Beer
**Typesetter:** Deirdre Geldenhuys
**Proofreader:** Inês Ferreira

Reproduction by Dominic Robson
Printed and bound in China by Golden Prosperity Printing & Packaging (Heyuan) Co., Ltd.

All rights reserved. No part of this publication may be reproduced, stored in a retrieval system, or transmitted, in any form or by any means, electronic, mechanical, photocopying, recording or otherwise, without the prior written permission of the copyright owner(s).

ISBN 978 1 77584 881 3 (Print)
ISBN 978 1 77584 882 0 (ePub)

**Front cover:** Woodland Kingfisher;
**Back cover, top to bottom:** White-bellied Sunbird, Saddle-billed Stork, Bateleur (Michael Mason), Eurasian Golden Oriole (Marc – stock.adobe.com), Pied Avocet;
**Title page:** Southern White-faced Owl;
**Contents page:** Southern Carmine Bee-eater

Making illegal copies of this publication, distributing them unlawfully or sharing them on social media without the written permission of the publisher may lead to civil claims or criminal complaints.
Protect the communities who are sustained by creativity.

## ACKNOWLEDGEMENTS

I would like to thank the many photographers who have contributed to this book. I understand just how time-consuming the process of photo gathering can be, and really appreciate the efforts everyone went to. In particular, I would like to thank Michael Mason, Mike Buckham, Daniel Engelbrecht, and Cliff and Suretha Dorse, as well as Adam Buckham, Andrew Walker, Jaime Rollinson, Nikos Petrou, Patrick O'Brien, Patrick Rollinson, Paul Rollinson and Rainer Summers, who have provided so many fantastic images, which have greatly improved this guide.

I am grateful to my wife, Jaime, for putting up with my many long hours and weekends working on the book, and appreciate the support she provided along the way. Also, to my parents, Paul and Helen, who have fostered my love of the outdoors and nature.

I would like to thank the team at Penguin Random House, especially Colette Alves, who I have worked closely with throughout this project, and Pippa Parker, who originally approached me with the idea of writing this guide.

# CONTENTS

| | |
|---|---|
| Introduction | 4 |
| Top birding sites in Botswana | 6 |
| Vegetation zones of Botswana | 8 |
| How to use this book | 10 |
| Glossary | 12 |
| Parts of a bird | 13 |
| **Species accounts** | 14 |
| Indexes | 135 |
|   Scientific names | 135 |
|   Setswana names | 139 |
|   Common names | 141 |

# INTRODUCTION

Botswana is a land of strong contrasts, from the red sands of the harsh Kalahari Desert to the swamps of the abundant Okavango system. This landlocked country is a wildlife haven that has welcomed and inspired outdoor travellers, wildlife enthusiasts, and birders alike.

Most of Botswana is dominated by the beautiful but unforgiving Kalahari Desert. *Kalahari* is derived from the Setswana word '*kgala*', which means 'the great thirst', and species that survive in this tough environment are specially adapted to a life with little water. Conversely, the Kalahari Desert truly comes alive in the summer months, when the area receives relatively large amounts of rain (mostly in the form of thunderstorms), drawing in high numbers of nomadic birds and other animals. The Kalahari influences vegetation across most of Botswana, with arid shrublands persisting in the southwest, while the central parts are dominated by bush and tree savanna.

Slaty Egret

On the other end of the spectrum, the lush and abundant Okavango system is teeming with life year-round, and is a sanctuary for birds and wildlife and a vital destination for migrating waterbirds. The Okavango Delta, a UNESCO World Heritage Site, is an inland delta formed by the Okavango River, which fans out into a massive, flat trough, creating a dynamic series of papyrus-lined channels, swamps and lagoons. During the Quaternary, the Okavango Delta linked up with the Makgadikgadi Pans, which are now a complex of alkaline flats and salt pans that usually hold no standing water. Only during exceptionally wet years does water from the Okavango reach the salt pans, which then come alive with breeding waterbirds, most notably flamingos.

Several large rivers flow through or border Botswana, and it is along these that many bird species' distributions further extend into Botswana, allowing them to persist in otherwise unsuitable habitat. Some of the country's major rivers include the Okavango, Kwando, Linyanti, Chobe and Limpopo.

Protected areas represent almost 30% of the country, the highest percentage in Africa, with some of the major protected areas including Kgalagadi Transfrontier Park, Central Kalahari Game Reserve, Makgadikgadi Pans National Park, Nxai Pan National Park, Moremi Game Reserve, Chobe National Park and Chobe Forest Reserve.

Burchell's Sandgrouse

# INTRODUCTION

## National Parks of Botswana

Birds may be found throughout the above-mentioned habitats and protected areas, with bird species diversity the lowest in the southwest in the arid shrublands of the Kalahari Desert. Bird species richness is the highest in the northeast, where the lush Zambezi woodlands (named after the Zambezi River, which does not flow into Botswana) are found. The area between the Kalahari Desert and the Zambezi woodlands is a transition zone where a mix of bird species typical of these two major zones occur.

Botswana is one of the premier birding destinations in Africa, with a bird list of around 600 species. Although the country has no endemic birds, it does have one near-endemic, the Slaty Egret, and is perhaps the best country to find the highly sought-after Pel's Fishing Owl.

This guide features 363 species, focusing on those that are common or likely to be encountered, while also including some of the more elusive birds that are most likely to be seen in Botswana.

Pel's Fishing Owl

# TOP BIRDING SITES IN BOTSWANA

Botswana has many varied and exciting birding sites, where a great number of the species mentioned in this guide can be found. Some of the country's top areas for birding are discussed below, including the special species that can be found there.

## Okavango Delta

This massive inland delta, including the panhandle to the north, Moremi Game Reserve along the eastern edge and the delta itself, offers some of the country's finest birding. The best way to experience the Okavango Delta is to take a boat trip through the area's vast network of channels, lagoons and bays. The delta is a waterbird haven, and hosts some of the country's most sought-after bird species, most notably Slaty Egret and Pel's Fishing Owl. Other standout species include White-backed Night Heron, Rufous-bellied Heron, African Pygmy Goose, Wattled Crane, African Skimmer, Long-toed Lapwing, Lesser Jacana, Coppery-tailed Coucal and Chirping Cisticola. The adjoining woodlands and riparian forest play host to Dickinson's Kestrel, Bradfield's Hornbill, Hartlaub's Babbler, Swamp Boubou and Brown Firefinch.

Long-toed Lapwing

## Chobe National Park

Although best known for its prime game-viewing opportunities, Chobe National Park has the highest bird species richness of any area in Botswana and boasts a stellar cast of highly desired specials. This wildlife haven protects large tracts of important tall woodlands, which host species such as Southern Ground and Bradfield's hornbills, Arnot's Chat and Retz's Helmetshrike. Other specials, such as Verreaux's Eagle-Owl, Broad-billed Roller, Swamp Boubou and Brown Firefinch, occur in riparian forest. A boat trip along the Chobe River offers the best viewing opportunities for the area's waterbirds, which include Slaty Egret, Long-toed Lapwing, Coppery-tailed Coucal, African Skimmer and Chirping Cisticola.

## Lake Ngami

Fed by the Okavango River system in especially wet years, the massive, seasonally flooded Lake Ngami (roughly 100 kilometres southwest of Maun) is an important site for waterfowl and waterbirds. Access may be tricky during particularly wet years, which is when the lake holds water, but those adventurous birders who step off the beaten path may be treated to large numbers of waterbirds, with a high potential for finding rare vagrants, such as Western Marsh Harrier and Lesser Black-backed Gull.

African Pygmy Goose

Pygmy FalconLesser Flamingo

## Makgadikgadi Pans

The Makgadikgadi Pans are a collection of salt pans (the largest being Sua, Ntwetwe and Nxai pans), surrounded by the Kalahari Desert. In birding circles, the pans are best known for their large numbers of breeding Greater and Lesser flamingos, which breed on Sua Pan during exceptionally wet years. Makgadikgadi also supports large numbers of waders (both migratory and resident species) and is the only reliable site for spotting Chestnut-banded Plover in Botswana. Other important waterbird species found here include Red-billed and Blue-billed teals, Great White Pelican, Saddle-billed Stork, Black Heron and Whiskered Tern. The low shrubland surrounding the pans hosts the likes of Secretarybird, Kori Bustard, Double-banded Courser, Burchell's Sandgrouse and Eastern Clapper Lark.

## Central Kalahari Game Reserve

This vast and seldom-visited game reserve is generally not on the radar for most visiting birders. However, it does afford adventurous birders the opportunity to view some fine Kalahari specials in a pristine setting. Central Kalahari Game Reserve is best accessed in four-wheel-drive vehicles, and each birding excursion should be planned carefully, as the area is extremely remote. Species to look out for in the reserve include Caspian Plover, Red-necked Falcon, Greater Kestrel, Temminck's and Double-banded coursers, and Rufous-eared Warbler.

## Kgalagadi Transfrontier Park

This park is part of a transboundary protected area, shared with South Africa. Although most visitors enter from the South African side, the Botswanan side offers a similar selection of species, with more space and tranquillity to enjoy viewing both game and arid-zone bird specials. Some of the park's noteworthy species include Pygmy and Red-footed falcons, Secretarybird, Kori Bustard, Burchell's and Namaqua sandgrouse, Southern White-faced Owl, Verreaux's Eagle-Owl, among others.

# VEGETATION ZONES OF BOTSWANA

- Deserts and xeric shrublands
- Tropical and subtropical grasslands, savannas and shrublands
- Flooded grasslands and savannas
- Salt pans
- Zambezi woodlands

This map shows the five major vegetation biomes found across Botswana. Many bird distributions are defined by these biomes, and sometimes fairly accurately follow similar divisions.

## Deserts and xeric shrublands
This biome is mostly restricted to the central and southwestern parts of the country and is characterised by low shrub vegetation and sparse tree cover in arid and semi-arid environments. It includes the Kalahari xeric savanna, with large trees mostly restricted to sandy ridges and dry riverbeds.

Kalahari shrublands

## Tropical and subtropical grasslands, savannas and shrublands
Covering most of the northeastern half of the country, this biome includes many transition habitats, which are characterised by a mostly open tree canopy and a heavy understorey of grass. Dense riparian forest exists along the perennial rivers in this biome, along which many 'wetter-country' species persist.

Kalahari grasslands

Floodplain, Okavango

## Flooded grasslands and savannas

This biome is seasonally or permanently flooded, and is centred around the lush Okavango Delta system in the northwest. The permanently flooded areas contain semi-aquatic vegetation, such as papyrus and sedges, while islands in between these flooded areas support dense swamp forests.

## Salt pans

Centred around the Makgadikgadi Pans, this biome supports low and sparse salt-tolerant shrubland and grassland. The pans themselves are devoid of any vegetation and only support life when they become temporarily flooded in exceptionally wet years.

Salt lake, Makgadikgadi Pans

## Zambezi woodlands

These woodlands are found in the extreme northeast of Botswana and support a dense and tall tree canopy with a sparse understorey. Miombo woodland (dominated by *Brachystegia* and *Julbernardia* species) is the dominant woodland type of this biome. Dense riparian forest exists along the perennial rivers such as the Kwando, Linyanti and Chobe rivers.

Zambezi woodlands

# HOW TO USE THIS BOOK

This lightweight, practical guide has been designed primarily for quick identification in the field, but it is also an ideal book to consult prior to your Botswana adventure. By looking at the photographs in advance, you will find it easier to identify species when you encounter them.

When using this book in the field, compare the bird's physical characteristics to the photographs and species description in the guide, and check if the bird is likely to be found in the area you are in by consulting the distribution map, as well as the status and habitat text.

## Features of each species account

1. **Photographs** depict useful identification features that are referred to in the text. Unless otherwise specified, photographs depict adults. For some species more than one photograph has been included to illustrate differences in plumage between sexes, ages, breeding stages, morphs or subspecies.

2. **Common and scientific names** in this guide follow the taxonomy in the International Ornithological Congress's World Bird List (version 14.2, August 2024).

3. **Size** indicates the average length of the bird, from the tip of the bill to the end of the tail. Where the breeding male develops a much longer tail, the measurement is given separately.

4. **Distribution maps** show where the species occurs in Botswana, and whether it is common or uncommon, a resident, migrant or vagrant.
   **dark green** = common resident, **light green** = uncommon resident,
   **dark red** = common migrant, **light red** = uncommon migrant,
   **red cross** = vagrant

5. **Species descriptions** are concise, highlighting the most diagnostic features in italics, and detailing plumage differences. Where confusion is possible, similar species are referenced. Voice is described only if it is an obvious or important identification feature.

6. **Status and habitat** indicates the bird's abundance in the region, and describes the type of vegetation in which it occurs.

7. **Setswana name**, where known.

## Abbreviations and symbols used in this book

ad. = **adult**
br. = **breeding**
non-br. = **non-breeding**

imm. = **immature**
juv. = **juvenile**
♂ = **male**   ♀ = **female**

# GLOSSARY

**Barred** (of plumage) Having alternate dark and light fine bands.
**Brood parasite** A bird that lays its egg in the nest of another species (host), relying on the host to raise the chicks.
**Call** Short notes that are usually made for contact or to signal danger.
**Cap** The area on top of the head, encompassing the forehead and crown.
**Casque** A horny or bony ridge on the top of the bill or head.
**Cere** A fleshy (often brightly coloured) covering at the base of the upper mandible of some birds (mostly raptors).
**Colonial** Associating in small groups, usually for breeding or roosting.
**Decurved** (of a bird's bill) Downward curving.
**Display** A courtship performance (including vocalisations and visual cues) given by male birds to attract females for mating.
**Endemic** Found solely in one area.
**Ephemeral** (of water bodies) Lasting for a short while (usually forming after rains).
**Eye-ring** A thin circle of feathers surrounding the eye.
**Flight feathers** The long primary and secondary feathers that enable flight.
**Flush** To startle a bird, driving it out from its cover.
**Frons** The forehead of a bird.
**Gape** Brightly coloured fleshy extension of the closed mandibles of a bird (often most obvious in young birds).
**Gorget** A patch of distinctive colouring on the throat.
**Immature** A bird between juvenile and adult plumages.
**Intra-African migrant** A species that spends part of its life cycle (breeding or wintering) in other parts of Africa.
**Juvenile** A young bird in its first fully acquired plumage after fledging.
**Loral spot** A spot immediately in front of the eye.
**Lores** The area immediately in front of the eye.
**Malar stripe** A stripe on the cheek.
**Migrant** A species that spends part of its life cycle (breeding or wintering) in other, more distant areas.
**Morph** A different colour variant found within a species.
**Mottled** (of plumage) Having spots or blotches of different colours.
**Moustachial stripe** A stripe running from the base of the bill down the side of the throat.
**Nape** The back of the neck.
**Near-endemic** Having most of the population in one area.
**Nuchal** Relating to the nape (often when describing a collar or patch).
**Onomatopoeic** (of a word) Derived from a sound.
**Palaearctic migrant** A species that spends part of its life cycle (breeding or wintering) in Europe or northern Asia.
**Plumage** The collective term for the feathers covering a bird.
**Plumes** Long, thin feathers used for display purposes; usually found on the head or back of large waterbirds.
**Primaries** The long flight feathers on the outer wing.
**Range** The area a species occupies during its lifetime.
**Raptor** A bird of prey.
**Resident** A species that does not perform any long-distance migration to reach its breeding or wintering grounds, occurring in an area year-round.
**Rictal bristles** The strong bristle-like feathers at the base of a bird's bill.
**Riparian** (of habitat) Associated with rivers.
**Scalloped** (of plumage patterning) Having curved or U-shaped markings.
**Secondaries** The long flight feathers on the inner wing, adjacent to the primaries.
**Shield** A bare bony patch on the forehead at the base of the bill; often brightly coloured.

**Song** A series of melodious notes used to defend territories and attract mating partners.
**Speculum** A patch of brightly coloured feathers on the secondaries; mostly found in ducks.
**Streaked** (of plumage) Having thin, short stripes.
**Subspecies** A geographical population of a species that is often distinctly different.
**Summer visitor** A species that spends time in an area only during the summer months.
**Supercilium** An eyebrow stripe.
**Vent** The feathered area under the tail of a bird.
**Wader** A normally long-legged species that forages in shallow water; also known as a shorebird.
**Wattle** A pendulous, fleshy protrusion normally on the head or neck of a bird.

## PARTS OF A BIRD

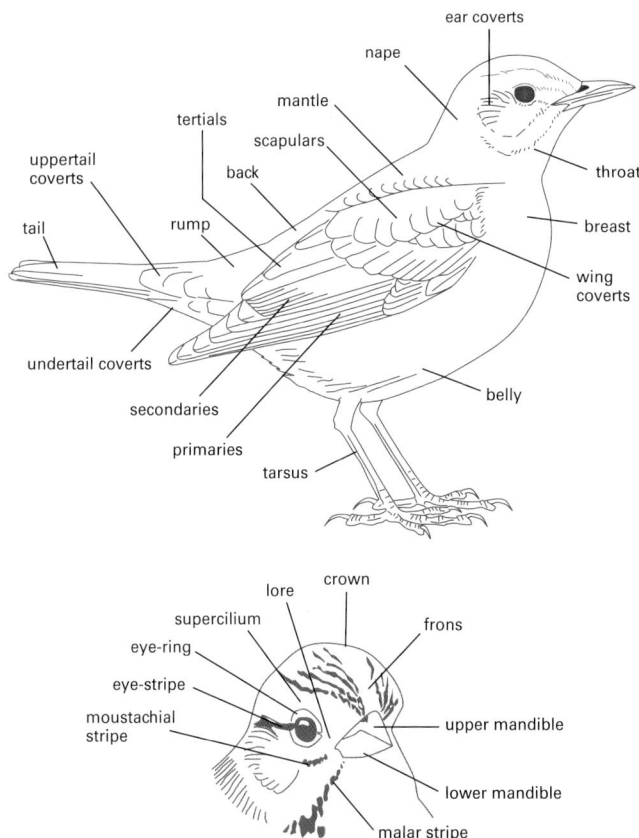

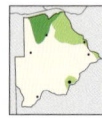

### Great White Pelican
*Pelecanus onocrotalus*

**140–178 cm** A large, mostly white waterbird with long yellow-and-pink bill and fleshy pouch. Male is larger and longer-billed than female. Similar to Pink-backed Pelican, but larger, with *crisper white plumage and lack of dark loral spot*; best separated in flight by *strongly contrasting underwings* (white underwing coverts with black flight feathers). **Status and habitat:** Common br. resident at water bodies across northern parts. SETSWANA: LE.YA

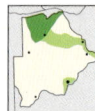

### Pink-backed Pelican
*Pelecanus rufescens*

**125–140 cm** A greyish-white pelican with a long, pinkish-yellow bill, *dark loral spot* in front of the eye, and a shaggy grey crest (most obvious in br. ad.). Pink back evident only in br. plumage and generally difficult to see. Sexes similar, but male larger. Similar to Great White Pelican, but smaller, with greyer plumage; best separated in flight by more uniform underwings. **Status and habitat:** Uncommon br. resident at water bodies. SETSWANA: LE.YA

Patrick Rollinson

### African Spoonbill    *Platalea alba*

**75–92 cm** A white waterbird with unique *spoon-shaped pink-red bill, pink-red facial skin* and legs, and white eyes. Juv. like ad., but with dark grey bill and facial skin, greyish-pink legs and dark eyes. Feeds by swinging bill from side to side, snapping up prey items. **Status and habitat:** Common br. resident in most water bodies, including wetlands, dams, lakes, floodplains and sewage works. SETSWANA: MMALESWANA

## African Sacred Ibis
*Threskiornis aethiopicus*

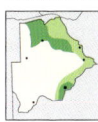

**65–89 cm** *A tall, mostly white ibis with naked black head and neck,* strongly decurved black bill, and *black wingtips and plumes on lower back*. Juv. and imm. like adult, but head and neck feathered, with white speckling. **Status and habitat:** Common br. resident in wetlands, floodplains, dams, pans (both permanent and ephemeral) and sewage works. Also enters cultivated fields and regularly scavenges at landfill sites. **SETSWANA: KÔKÔLÔHUTWE**

## Hadada Ibis *Bostrychia hagedash*

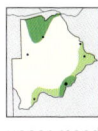

**76–85 cm** *A medium-sized, relatively short-necked, mostly dark grey ibis* with iridescent upperwing coverts, dark, decurved bill with red base to upper mandible. Southern subspecies paler grey, with dark eyes. *Voice loud, raucous; the blaring 'HA-DA-DA' when calling as a group can be ear-splitting.* **Status and habitat:** Common to uncommon br. resident of the Okavango system and extreme northeast, and along the Limpopo River. Found in moist open country such as grassland, agricultural fields, woodland and suburbia. **SETSWANA: TSHABABARWA**

## Glossy Ibis *Plegadis falcinellus*

**49–66 cm** *A sleek, long-necked ibis with chestnut and iridescent green and purple plumage,* strongly decurved grey bill, bare dark lores with pale bluish-white borders and long legs. Non-br. ad. and juv. have white streaking to head and neck. **Status and habitat:** Common to uncommon br. resident. Strongly tied to aquatic habitats, including wetlands, permanent and ephemeral pans, marshes and sewage works. **SETSWANA: NAME UNKNOWN**

## Hamerkop
*Scopus umbretta*

**50–58 cm** An unusual all-brown waterbird *with distinct crest feathers forming hammer-shaped head* ('hamerkop' means 'hammerhead' in Afrikaans) and longish legs. Voice a loud, excited yelp '*kip-kip-kip*' and various squawks, mostly given from trees and in flight. Pairs build a massive domed-structure nest of sticks and twigs; usually built in trees. **Status and habitat:** Common br. resident found on the edges of pans, dams, lakes and rivers, with large trees nearby. **SETSWANA: MMAMASILOANOKA**

## Greater Flamingo
*Phoenicopterus roseus*

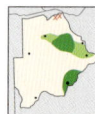

**125–165 cm** A tall, long-legged, long-necked waterbird with dull pink to white plumage, and *contrasting two-toned bill*. Bright pink wing coverts with dark flight feathers appear striking in flight. Young birds lack pink plumage, with grey (not pink) legs and grey bills. Smaller Lesser Flamingo has darker bill and brighter pink plumage. **Status and habitat:** Breeds in large numbers in salt pans in Makgadikgadi Pans (Sua Pan), dispersing to dams and sewage works in non-br. season. **SETSWANA: MO.GÔLÔRI**

## Lesser Flamingo
*Phoeniconaias minor*

**90–125 cm** Smaller than Greater Flamingo, with *brighter pink plumage and black-tipped dark red bill*. Black flight feathers contrast with deep pink wing coverts in flight. Juv. is dirty grey-brown, lacking any pink coloration, with a dark grey bill. **Status and habitat:** Breeds in Sua Pan (Makgadikgadi Pans), dispersing to dams and sewage works in non-br. season. **SETSWANA: MO.GÔLÔRI**

HERONS, BITTERN

### Black-crowned Night Heron
*Nycticorax nycticorax*

**54–60 cm** *A medium-sized, stocky heron with white underparts, grey upperwings, black crown and back,* black bill, red eyes and yellow legs. Juv. brown-grey with white-spotted upperparts and heavily streaked pale underparts. Similar to juv. White-backed Night Heron and juv. Striated Heron (p. 18). **Status and habitat:** Common resident and local nomad in rivers, lakes and other aquatic habitats with overhanging trees or reeds. **SETSWANA: NAME UNKNOWN**

### White-backed Night Heron
*Calherodius leuconotus*

**50–56 cm** A small heron with *black head, large dark eyes, with obvious pale eye-ring, chestnut neck,* grey-brown back and wings, and yellow legs. *White back patch* obvious only during courtship display and in flight. Juv. paler with pale- and dark-streaked underparts and white upperwing spots. Like juv. Black-crowned Night Heron, but has longer neck and darker crown, bill and eyes. **Status and habitat:** Uncommon to rare resident of dense vegetation along rivers and swamps. **SETSWANA: NAME UNKNOWN**

### Dwarf Bittern
*Botaurus sturmii*

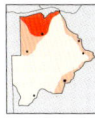

**26–30 cm** A *small* dark bittern with *charcoal upperparts, heavily streaked pale underparts, dull yellow legs,* and bare bluish-green lores. Juv. duller and paler, with buff-tipped feathers to upperparts. Ad. superficially similar to larger Striated Heron (p. 18), but has uniform upperparts (lacking darker crown) and dull yellow (not orange-yellow) legs. **Status and habitat:** Uncommon intra-African br. summer migrant occurring in temporary well-vegetated pans and pools. May be particularly common and widespread in wet years. **SETSWANA: KGAPU**

HERONS

### Striated Heron  *Butorides striata*

**40–44 cm** *A small, dark heron with grey underparts, mostly grey-green upperparts, dark crown,* long black bill with yellow base to lower mandible, and orange-yellow eyes, lores and legs. Juv. like Dwarf Bittern (p. 17) and juv. Black-crowned Night Heron (p. 17), but has darkly streaked underparts and white-spotted dark upperparts; separated by longer, thinner bill, bright yellow (not dull green) lores and plainer upperparts. **Status and habitat:** Common br. resident of rivers, lakes, dams and other aquatic habitats with dense vegetation. **SETSWANA: NAME UNKNOWN**

### Squacco Heron  *Ardeola ralloides*

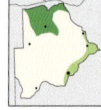

**42–46 cm** *A small, buff-coloured heron with bright white wings, which contrast with darker body in flight,* white underparts, dark-tipped blue bill, and dull yellow legs. Non-br. ad. and juv. have heavily streaked chest, neck and head, darker upperparts and green-yellow bill base. **Status and habitat:** Common br. resident of well-vegetated or reed-lined water bodies.
**SETSWANA: NAME UNKNOWN**

### Grey Heron  *Ardea cinerea*

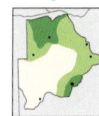

**90–100 cm** A medium-sized, mostly grey heron with *pale head, black head plumes,* and orange to light grey-yellow bill and legs. Similar to Black-headed Heron, but has light grey head, face and neck and all-grey underwings (visible in flight). Juv. like ad. but darker grey overall with dark grey crown. **Status and habitat:** Common br. resident along shorelines of most aquatic habitats. **SETSWANA: SE.NGWÊPÊ**

## Black-headed Heron
*Ardea melanocephala*

**86–94 cm** A medium-sized *dark grey heron with black-and-white neck*, head and underwings, and dark grey to black bill and legs. Juv. has dark grey head and neck. **Status and habitat:** Uncommon br. resident in open terrestrial habitats, including grassland, fields and agricultural areas. Rarely seen feeding at the edge of aquatic habitats; the *non-aquatic counterpart of Grey Heron.* SETSWANA: KÔKÔLÔFUTÊ

## Goliath Heron
*Ardea goliath*

**135–150 cm** *A massive heron with dark grey upperparts, chestnut head, neck and belly*, white chin and throat with black streaks lower down neck, and dark grey bill and legs. Superficially similar to much smaller Purple Heron, but differs in face, crown and neck patterning, and leg and bill colour. **Status and habitat:** Common br. resident mostly restricted to the Okavango system in aquatic habitats, including rivers, wetlands, marshes and floodplains. SETSWANA: NAME UNKNOWN

## Purple Heron
*Ardea purpurea*

**78–90 cm** A medium-sized heron with *grey-purple upperparts,* light chestnut neck and underparts, *black crown, black stripes on neck and face, and yellow bill and legs.* Similar to Goliath Heron, but considerably smaller, with black stripes on head and neck. **Status and habitat:** Common br. resident mostly restricted to aquatic habitats with dense vegetation cover and reed beds of the Okavango system. SETSWANA: NAME UNKNOWN

HERONS, EGRET

### Rufous-bellied Heron
*Ardeola rufiventris*

**38–40 cm** A medium-sized *mostly sooty heron with rufous lower belly, inner wings and tail*, dark-tipped yellow bill and lores, and yellow legs. Juv. duller with pale-streaked underparts. Ad. superficially similar to taller and slimmer Slaty Egret but has yellow (not dark) bill and rufous belly, wings and tail. **Status and habitat:** Uncommon resident of flooded grassland, reed beds and swamps. SETSWANA: NAME UNKNOWN

### Black Heron
*Egretta ardesiaca*

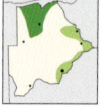

**50–60 cm** *A slate-grey heron with bright yellow feet*, with elongated crown, mantle and chest plumes. Juv. lacks plumes. Crouches low over water with wings covering head in *unique 'umbrella' fishing method*. Often gregarious when foraging. Similar to Slaty Egret, but plumage generally darker, lacks chestnut throat patch, with dark (not yellow) legs. **Status and habitat:** Uncommon br. resident favouring shallow water bodies, such as lakes, rivers, marshes and floodplains. SETSWANA: SE.KHUKO

### Slaty Egret
*Egretta vinaceigula*

**45–60 cm** A dark grey egret with *chestnut throat patch* and *all-yellow legs*. Similar to Black Heron, but slimmer and longer-necked, with pale eyes, and does not 'umbrella' forage. Superficially similar to Rufous-bellied Heron. **Status and habitat:** Uncommon and localised br. resident restricted to the Okavango system and extreme northeast. Favours shallow wetland edges and floodplains. SETSWANA: NAME UNKNOWN

## Great Egret
*Ardea alba*

**85–95 cm** *A tall, long-necked egret with entirely white plumage, and black bill, legs and feet.* Non-br. ad. and juv. have yellow bill; may be confused with Yellow-billed Egret, but taller with longer neck and gape extending beyond eye. **Status and habitat:** Common br. resident, occurring in aquatic habitats, including rivers, lakes, marshes, floodplains and dams. SETSWANA: MO.GÔLÔRI

## Yellow-billed Egret *Ardea brachyrhyncha*

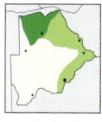

**65–72 cm** A white egret with yellow bill (orange-red in br. ad.) *with short gape*, and black legs, often with pale yellow thighs. *Smaller and shorter-necked than Great Egret.* May be confused with Western Cattle Egret (p. 22), which is smaller with shorter neck. **Status and habitat:** Common br. resident. Occurs in aquatic habitats including wetlands, marshes and floodplains.
SETSWANA: MO.LEANE

## Little Egret
*Egretta garzetta*

**55–65 cm** A long-necked egret with white plumage, long plumes on head, mantle and breast, *black legs with chrome-yellow feet*, black bill and orange to purple lores. Non-br. ad. has green lores, and lacks plumes. **Status and habitat:** Common br. resident favouring edges of wetlands, marshes, rivers and dams. SETSWANA: MMAMOLEANE

## Western Cattle Egret *Ardea ibis*

**48–54 cm** *A small, white egret with orange mantle, chest, nape and crown,* cream-yellow legs, lores and eyes, and orange-red bill. Non-br. ad. mostly lacks orange plumage, legs darker. Juv. with black bill and legs. Often forages beside large herbivores, snatching disturbed prey items. Like Yellow-billed Egret (p. 21), but with orange plumage; mostly avoids aquatic habitats (except when breeding or roosting). **Status and habitat:** Common and widespread br. resident in open habitats, including fields, savanna and agricultural land. **SETSWANA: MO.LEANE**

## African Openbill *Anastomus lamelligerus*

**74–90 cm** *An all-dark stork with a slight glossy sheen to plumage and unique open-bill shape*, designed to aid in removal of snails and other molluscs from their shells. Juv. like ad., but lacks glossy sheen, has paler tips to feathers and a reduced gap in the bill. **Status and habitat:** Common br. resident and nomad of the Okavango system and northeast. Occurs in most freshwater bodies, including wetlands, marshes, dams and ephemeral pans. **SETSWANA: LE.KÔLÔLWANE**

## Marabou Stork *Leptoptilos crumenifer*

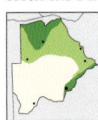

**130–152 cm** *A large stork with a bald, pink-red head, pendulous pink throat pouch,* grey-black upperparts, white ruff and belly, and long, pale bill. In flight, shows mostly dark grey underwings with white inner wing spurs, extending from belly; massive wingspan. **Status and habitat:** Common br. resident and nomad in a variety of open habitats, from woodland to grassland, as well as wetland edges, dams and rivers. Scavenges at refuse dumps, and at carcasses with vultures. **SETSWANA: GHUBÊ**

## Yellow-billed Stork  *Mycteria ibis*

**95–105 cm** A large stork with *bright yellow bill, bare red facial skin* and legs, white plumage with pinkish tinge, and black flight feathers and tail. Juv. light grey-brown. Superficially similar to White Stork, but has bare facial skin and yellow bill. **Status and habitat:** Common br. resident and summer visitor, which occurs in a variety of aquatic habitats. SETSWANA: LE.KÔLLWANE

## White Stork  *Ciconia ciconia*

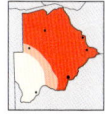

**100–125 cm** A large, *easily recognisable stork with red bill and legs, and mostly white plumage with black flight feathers*. Juv. like ad., but has dark bill, brown-red legs and light brown upperwings. Similar to Yellow-billed Stork. **Status and habitat:** Common Palearctic-br. summer migrant. Found in most open habitats, such as grassland, floodplains, cultivated fields and open woodland, where it may occur in large feeding flocks. SETSWANA: LE.KÔLÔLWANE

## Abdim's Stork  *Ciconia abdimii*

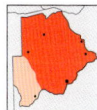

**76–81 cm** A small, dark stork with *white belly, blue-and-red naked facial skin, pale grey bill*, grey legs, and red 'knee' joints and feet. In flight, shows white lower back patch. Juv. like ad., but browner and duller. **Status and habitat:** Common non-br. summer visitor found in terrestrial habitats, including fields, grassland, savannas and even semi-arid areas. SETSWANA: LE.KÔLÔLWANE

STORKS, DARTER

### African Woolly-necked Stork
*Ciconia microscelis*

**80–90 cm** A medium-sized stork with *white neck*, dark-mottled face, iridescent dark back, wings and chest, and *white lower belly and tail*. Unlikely to be confused with other storks due to combination of white neck with dark body. **Status and habitat:** Common but localised resident, mostly restricted to Okavango system and Chobe National Park. Occurs in and around wetlands, floodplains and swamp forests. **SETSWANA: LE.KÔLLWANE**

### Saddle–billed Stork
*Ephippiorhynchus senegalensis*

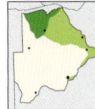

**145-150 cm** A tall, striking black-and-white stork *with red-and-black bill with yellow 'saddle'*, and dark legs with red 'knees'. In flight, shows white flight feathers with black underwing coverts. Male has dark eyes with yellow wattles; female has pale yellow eyes, without wattles. Juv. lacks yellow 'saddle' on bill, and has grey belly and upper mantle and brown-black neck. **Status and habitat:** Uncommon br. resident found in wetlands, pans and along large rivers. **SETSWANA: MO.LÔMBWE**

### African Darter     *Anhinga rufa*

**80–95 cm** A large cormorant-like waterbird with *long, thin rufous-brown neck with white lateral stripe, long tail* and brown-black breast and belly. Routinely glides, when broad wings and long tail are evident. Forages in water with only head and neck visible, recalling a snake. Dries plumage by sitting with wings held open. Confusion likely only with Reed Cormorant. **Status and habitat:** Common br. resident found at water bodies, mostly restricted to the Okavango system. **SETSWANA: TIMÊLÊTSANE**

## White-breasted Cormorant
*Phalacrocorax lucidus*

**85–95 cm** A large dark brown-black cormorant with *white throat and chest*, dull yellow skin at base of lower mandible, and white patch on lower flanks. Non-br. ad. and juv. with entirely white underparts. Juv. similar to much smaller juv. Reed Cormorant, but with longer bill and proportionately shorter tail. **Status and habitat:** Common localised resident in large open water bodies, such as dams and large rivers.
SETSWANA: TIMÊLÊTSANE

## Reed Cormorant  *Microcarbo africanus*

**50–60 cm** *A small cormorant with short orange-yellow bill*, orange-red bare facial skin, *slight crest, longish tail*, and black plumage with contrasting grey upperwings. Non-br. ad. and juv. browner above and cream-white below (especially throat), with cream yellow facial skin, lacking crest. Often sits with wings open to dry plumage. Similar to much larger White-breasted Cormorant, as well as larger African Darter, but has crest, hook-tipped bill, and shorter neck. **Status and habitat:** Common br. resident in freshwater bodies. SETSWANA: TIMÊLÊTSANE

## Little Grebe  *Tachybaptus ruficollis*

**23–29 cm** A very small, mostly dark grebe with a *rich rufous neck and obvious white spot at base of black bill*. Non-br. ad. and imm. similar, with paler underparts, buff-brown neck and paler bill, which merges with white patch at bill base. Juv. has black-and-white-striped cheeks. Utters a high-pitched trill during br. season. **Status and habitat:** Common br. resident in ponds, lakes, dams and slow-moving rivers; may also be found in salt pans. SETSWANA: SE.NWÊDI

### White-faced Whistling Duck
*Dendrocygna viduata*

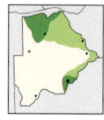

**44–48 cm** A fairly large, mostly dark brown duck with *white face and throat* and finely barred flanks. Similar to Fulvous Whistling Duck in shape and size, but overall darker brown, and lacks white crescent in uppertail. Juv. paler than adult, with dirty brown face and throat. Voice a high-pitched whistle; highly vocal. **Status and habitat:** Common br. resident in freshwater bodies. Highly gregarious and conspicuous; unlikely to be overlooked. SETSWANA: LE.WEWE, LE.WIIWII

### Fulvous Whistling Duck
*Dendrocygna bicolor*

**43–50 cm** A large duck with *cinnamon-brown head and underparts*, white-striped flanks, dark brown upperparts with scaling, and a white crescent in the uppertail (visible only in flight). Juv. paler and lacks scaling. Similar to White-faced Whistling Duck in size and shape, but paler and lacks white face. **Status and habitat:** Uncommon br. resident and nomad, depending on water levels. Occurs in freshwater; particularly abundant in the Okavango system. SETSWANA: SE.HUDI, SE.FUDI

### White-backed Duck
*Thalassornis leuconotus*

**38–43 cm** A small duck with buff-and-brown-barred plumage, distinctive *white patch at base of bill,* and white lower back, visible only in flight. Sits low in the water and is easily overlooked. **Status and habitat:** Common br. resident in the Okavango system; patchily distributed and nomadic elsewhere in the northeast. Frequents water lily-covered pans, wetlands and other small water bodies, where it commonly occurs alongside African Pygmy Goose (p. 28). SETSWANA: SE.HUDI, SE.FUDI

GEESE, DUCK 27

## Spur-winged Goose
*Plectropterus gambensis*

**75–100 cm** A large goose with *iridescent black plumage and varying amounts of white on face, neck, belly and forewings.* Bill, bare facial skin and legs pinkish-red. Imm. duller and browner than ad. **Status and habitat:** Common and conspicuous br. resident in verdant areas. Found in any freshwater body; frequently feeds in adjacent floodplains and agricultural land.
SETSWANA: LE.TSUKWÊ, SE.HUDI SÊSEFATSHWA

## Knob-billed Duck
*Sarkidiornis melanotos*

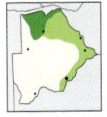

**56–76 cm** A large duck with white-and-dark-speckled head, *iridescent blue-black upperparts* and *white underparts.* Br. male has obvious *fleshy knob on bill* (reduced in non-br.); female lacks fleshy bill knob. Juv. mostly light brown and shows dark eye-stripe. **Status and habitat:** Common br. resident and occasional nomad; numbers are bolstered in summer from neighbouring countries. Found in freshwater bodies, particularly seasonal pans after heavy rains. SETSWANA: RANKÔ

## Egyptian Goose *Alopochen aegyptiaca*

**60–75 cm** A large, mostly light brown waterfowl with *dark eye patch, breast patch and neck collar,* pink legs and dark-tipped pink bill. In flight, shows *white wing coverts and iridescent green speculum patch,* contrasting with overall brown plumage. Juv. duller, and lacks dark breast patch, neck collar and eye patch. Makes loud, rasping honks and hisses. **Status and habitat:** Common br. resident. Conspicuous in freshwater bodies; grazes in urban habitats such as golf courses and playing fields. SETSWANA: LE.HARATHATA

### African Pygmy Goose *Nettapus auritus*

**30–33 cm** A very small duck with white face, *tawny-orange flanks and chest* and metallic green upperparts. In flight, shows white secondary patches. Male has *black-bordered green neck patch*, dark green crown and orange bill with dark tip. Female has dusky face and bill; lacks green neck patch. **Status and habitat:** Uncommon br. resident, mostly restricted to the Okavango system and other wetlands. Favours freshwater wetlands with floating vegetation, especially water lilies. SETSWANA: SE.HUDI, SE.HUTSANA

### Cape Shoveler *Spatula smithii*

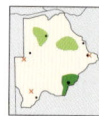

**48–54 cm** A medium-sized, mostly brown-grey duck with *black spatulate bill*, scalloped underparts, and white underwing coverts. Male has dark lower back, pale blue upperwing coverts, paler head, bright yellow eyes, and orange legs and feet. Female is more uniformly brown, with grey upperwing coverts, dark eyes, and brown legs and feet. **Status and habitat:** Common br. resident, mostly restricted to the southeast and the Makgadikgadi Pans. Found in shallow freshwater pans and saltpans. SETSWANA: SE.HUDI, SE.FUDI

### Blue-billed Teal *Spatula hottentota*

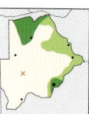

**32–36 cm** A very small duck with *black cap, creamy cheeks and bright blue bill*. Upperparts dark brown and underparts light brown with scalloping. Superficially resembles Red-billed Teal, but that species is larger with red (not blue) bill. **Status and habitat:** Fairly common br. resident in permanent and seasonal freshwater systems. Avoids large open expanses of water, preferring quieter bays with abundant floating vegetation. SETSWANA: SE.HUDI, SE.FUDI

TEALS, DUCK

## Cape Teal
*Anas capensis*

**44–48 cm** *A small pale grey teal with pink-red bill*, orange-red eyes, and dark-scalloped underparts. In flight, grey wings with contrasting white secondaries and green speculum patch obvious. Superficially similar to Red-billed Teal, but has plain pale grey (not black) crown. **Status and habitat:** Uncommon to locally common resident (and intra-African summer migrant) found in fresh- and saltwater habitats, including salt pans, dams, lakes and sewage works. **SETSWANA: SE.HUDI**

## Red-billed Teal
*Anas erythrorhyncha*

**43–48 cm** A medium-sized duck with a *black cap, red bill and tan-coloured cheek patches*, dark brown upperparts, and light brown scalloped underparts. Tan secondary patches, visible in flight, separate it from other ducks. Resembles Cape and Blue-billed (p. 28) teals, but latter species is smaller with a blue (not red) bill. **Status and habitat:** Common br. resident and nomad; most abundant in Okavango system and Lake Ngami. Prefers shallow wetlands but gathers at larger water bodies in non-br. season. **SETSWANA: SE.HUDI, SE.FUDI**

## Yellow-billed Duck
*Anas undulata*

**52–58 cm** Unmistakable, with *bright yellow bill with a dark saddle*, uniform grey-brown-scalloped plumage, and iridescent green speculum patch (most obvious in flight). Juv. less boldly scalloped below. **Status and habitat:** Br. resident that is scarce around the Okavango system and extreme northeast but more abundant in the southeast around Gaborone, where it frequents man-made dams and sewage works. Occurs in most freshwater bodies, avoiding fast-flowing rivers. **SETSWANA: SE.HUDI, SE.FUDI**

POCHARD, DUCK, VULTURE

## Southern Pochard
*Netta erythrophthalma*

**48–51 cm** An *all dark brown duck with blue-grey bill* and strong *white wing bar* (only evident in flight). *Female with obvious white crescent on face and neck*, and white at base of bill. Male superficially similar to male Maccoa Duck, but with darker brown coloration, duller grey (not bright blue) bill and much shorter tail. **Status and habitat:** Common to uncommon resident in large water bodies, such as dams, as well as wetlands and sewage works. **SETSWANA: SE.HUDI**

## Maccoa Duck
*Oxyura maccoa*

**48–51 cm** A distinctive duck with *chestnut body, black head, bright blue bill,* and *long, pointed tail*. Female and non-br. male dark brown with pale stripe below eye and pale throat. Male superficially similar to male Southern Pochard. **Status and habitat:** Uncommon to locally common resident in large, deep water bodies such as dams and lakes, also favouring sewage works. **SETSWANA: SE.HUDI**

## Hooded Vulture
*Necrosyrtes monachus*

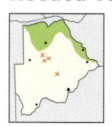

**65–75 cm** A smallish, *dark vulture with bare pink face and foreneck*, and *longish, thin bill*. In flight, shows mostly dark flight feathers with silvery undersides to secondary feathers. Juv. has pale grey face and foreneck. Similar plumage to much larger Lappet-faced Vulture, but has more delicate bill and lacks obvious white leggings. **Status and habitat:** Uncommon to common resident of woodland and moist savanna. **SETSWANA: MOTLHANKA-WAMANÔNG**

## White-backed Vulture  *Gyps africanus*

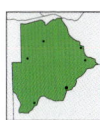

**90–100 cm** A large vulture with uniform light grey-brown plumage, mostly bare head and neck, and dark eyes. In flight, *black flight feathers, contrasting with white or pale underwing coverts, and white lower back evident.* Juv. has darker underwing coverts with pale bar. Can be confused with Cape Vulture, but has more contrast between underwing coverts and flight feathers. **Status and habitat:** Common, yet declining, widespread br. resident and nomad across open savanna. SETSWANA: **LE.NÔNG**

## Cape Vulture  *Gyps coprotheres*

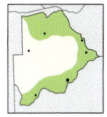

**100–120 cm** A very large buffy brown vulture with pale underwing coverts and *light grey-brown flight feathers*. Can be confused with White-backed Vulture but lacks white lower back and strong contrast in underwing coloration, and has pale (not dark) eyes. **Status and habitat:** Uncommon br. resident (breeding on cliffs) and nomad, foraging over woodland and savanna, avoiding the Kalahari Desert. SETSWANA: **LE.NÔNG**

## Lappet-faced Vulture
*Torgos tracheliotos*

**98–115 cm** A large, mostly *black-brown vulture* with *bare pink-red head and neck lappets*, white neck ruff, flanks and thighs, and yellowish bill. In flight, shows almost entirely black underwings with white carpal spurs. May be confused with smaller Hooded and White-headed vultures (p. 32). **Status and habitat:** Uncommon and widespread resident found in savanna and semi-arid areas. SETSWANA: **BIBING**

### White-headed Vulture
*Trigonoceps occipitalis*

**75–85 cm** A striking *black-and-white vulture* with dark upperparts and chest, *white head*, belly and leggings, *and red bill with pale blue base*. In flight, shows mostly dark underwings with silvery inner secondaries; secondaries crisp white in female. Juv. has uniformly dark brown-black plumage with dark cap. Juv. similar to larger juv. Lappet-faced Vulture (p. 31), but with reddish (not blackish-horn) bill tip. **Status and habitat:** Uncommon resident in savanna and dry woodland.
SETSWANA: **MOTLHANKA-WAMANÔNG**

### Secretarybird    *Sagittarius serpentarius*

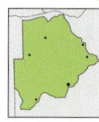

**125–150 cm** A distinctive, *large, long-legged raptor* with mostly grey plumage, black flight feathers and leggings, *long head plumes, orange facial skin* and barred tail with elongated central tail feathers. Juv. like ad., but has yellow facial skin and shorter tail. **Status and habitat:** Uncommon br. resident in open habitats including grassland, open savanna and semi-desert plains. SETSWANA: **RAMOLÔNGWANA**

### African Fish Eagle   *Icthyophaga vocifer*

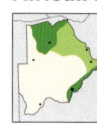

**63–73 cm** A large eagle with *pure white head, breast and tail*, contrasting with *deep chestnut underparts*, and slaty black upperparts and flight feathers. Imm. and juv. variably mottled, with white windows in primaries and white tail with black terminal band; becomes paler-headed with age. Voice a highly distinctive, far-carrying '*kyow-kow-kow*' cry. **Status and habitat:** Common br. resident *strongly associated with aquatic habitats*, occurring in high densities in the Okavango system.
SETSWANA: **KGOADIRA**

## Bateleur
*Terathopius ecaudatus*

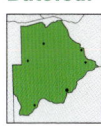

**55–70 cm** A striking, *mostly black eagle with bare red facial skin, cere and unfeathered legs,* large grey shoulder patches, rufous (or cream) mantle patch, and orange-yellow-based bill with dark tip. In flight, shows distinctive *black-and-white underwings* (male evenly black and white; female mostly white) *and very short tail*. Imm. and juv. uniformly brown, with grey-green legs, cere and bare facial skin. **Status and habitat:** Common to uncommon br. resident in open and closed savanna.
SETSWANA: PÊTLÊKÊ

## Martial Eagle
*Polemaetus bellicosus*

**76–86 cm** A large, heavyset eagle with *black-spotted white underparts and dark brown upperparts, chest and head (with short crest)*. Juv. has pale head and face and plain white underparts. Ad. like Black-chested Snake Eagle (p. 35), but larger, with crest, dark underwings, and spotted underparts.
**Status and habitat:** Uncommon br. resident throughout Botswana, where it is found in open savanna as well as semi-arid areas close to riverbeds with large trees.
SETSWANA: NTSU

## Tawny Eagle
*Aquila rapax*

**65–76 cm** A large brown eagle with variable plumage, most commonly *buff or light brown morphs*. Separated from Wahlberg's Eagle (p. 34) by shape: *at rest, shows larger head, lacking small crest, with heavy bill; in flight, shows broad, rounded wings and short, often round-ended tail;* pale patch sometimes on lower back. Similar to Lesser Spotted Eagle (p. 34), which has shorter tail, tightly feathered leggings, and rounded (not oval-shaped) nostrils. Juv. has pale rump and pale covert bar to upper- and underwings.
**Status and habitat:** Common br. resident in open savanna. SETSWANA: NTSU

### Lesser Spotted Eagle  *Clanga pomarina*

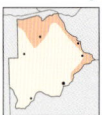

**58–65 cm** A medium-sized dark brown eagle with *tightly feathered legs*, relatively large head, and yellow cere with rounded nostrils. In flight, shows darker flight feathers contrasting with paler coverts, *double 'comma' marks at base of underwing primaries*, and white patch on lower back. Juv. has white-edged wing coverts and white rump. Like Tawny (p. 33) and Wahlberg's eagles, but has larger head, shorter tail and broader, rounder wings. **Status and habitat:** Uncommon non-br. summer migrant in savanna. **SETSWANA: NTSU**

pale morph    dark morph

### Wahlberg's Eagle  *Hieraaetus wahlbergi*

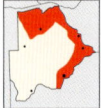

**55–60 cm** A medium-sized brown eagle with several colour morphs, mostly entirely dark brown; pale morph has cream-white head, neck and underparts with lightly scaled dark brown upperparts. Dark morph separated from Lesser Spotted and dark morph Booted eagles, while Tawny Eagle (p. 33) separated by shape: in flight, shows *long, straight wings with long, thin, square-ended tail*; at rest, shows smallish head (*often with slight crest*) and bill. **Status and habitat:** Common br. summer migrant in savanna and open woodland. **SETSWANA: NTSU**

### Booted Eagle  *Hieraaetus pennatus*

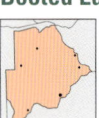

**45–55 cm** A smallish eagle found in *two distinct colour morphs*. Pale morph has *pale underparts with thinly streaked upper chest*; in flight, shows pale upperwing coverts, *white spots at the base of the leading edge of wings* (landing lights), and *pale uppertail coverts*. Dark morph has rufous-brown underparts. Similar to equivalent morphs of larger Wahlberg's Eagle, but with white 'landing lights' and pale uppertail coverts. **Status and habitat:** Uncommon br. summer migrant in savanna, open woodland, and shrubland. **SETSWANA: NTSU**

dark morph

## African Hawk-Eagle *Aquila spilogaster*

**60–68 cm** A large, distinctive eagle with *black upperparts, heavily streaked white underparts*, and yellow feet and cere. In flight, mostly white flight feathers (with black tips) contrast strongly with black coverts on upper- and underwings; tail finely barred black-and-white. Juv. with rufous underparts and head, and darker brown upperparts; may be confused with other brown eagles, but has similar wing pattern to ad., with coverts contrastingly rufous. **Status and habitat:** Uncommon br. resident in open savanna and woodland. **SETSWANA: NTSU**

## Black-chested Snake Eagle
*Circaetus pectoralis*

**63–68 cm** A large, dark brown-and-white snake eagle with large bright yellow eyes. Similar to Martial Eagle, *but smaller, lacks any black spots to white underparts, with mostly white underwings and unfeathered legs*. Juv. has plain buff-brown head and breast, with white-and-buff-scaled belly. **Status and habitat:** Uncommon resident across much of Botswana, occurring in open habitats, including savanna, grassland and semi-arid areas. **SETSWANA: SE.GÔDI**

## Brown Snake Eagle *Circaetus cinereus*

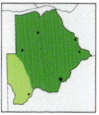

**70–75 cm** A large, mostly uniformly dark brown snake eagle with large bright yellow eyes, unfeathered grey legs and barred brown-and-white tail. In flight, shows *silver-grey underwing flight feathers contrasting with dark brown coverts*. Juv. like ad., but with white blotching to underparts; may be confused with juv. Black-chested Snake Eagle, but generally darker brown with shorter wings (barely projecting beyond tail tip at rest). **Status and habitat:** Uncommon br. resident found throughout Botswana in open savanna and other lightly wooded areas. **SETSWANA: SE.GÔDI**

HARRIER, KITE, HARRIER-HAWK

### African Marsh Harrier *Circus ranivorus*

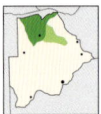

**44–50 cm** A mostly brown harrier with *heavily barred flight feathers* (above and below), *barred tail*, cream rump, ginger-brown underparts with dark streaks, and bare yellow legs and cere. *Typical harrier-like foraging style*, flying low and slowly over vegetation, dropping down onto prey. Juv. like ad., but darker brown and less obviously barred, often showing creamy chest bar and face, with dark crown. **Status and habitat:** Common br. resident across wetlands and other open habitat. **SETSWANA: SE.GÔDI**

### Yellow-billed Kite  *Milvus aegyptius*

**50–58 cm** A large, mostly brown raptor with *all-yellow bill and deeply forked tail* (most obvious in flight). Juv. has yellow cere with dark bill tip, and generally lighter underparts with dark streaking. Highly vocal when breeding, uttering a high-pitched, whinnying call. Distinguished from other local raptors by all-yellow bill. **Status and habitat:** A very common br. and non-br. summer migrant and local nomad, which may be found in most open habitats, including woodland, savanna, riparian forest, grassland and suburbia. **SETSWANA: MMANKGÔDI**

### African Harrier-Hawk
*Polyboroides typus*

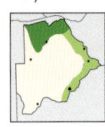

**60–66 cm** A large grey hawk with *broad wings*, black-tipped flight feathers, *black tail with broad white band*, *bare yellow (sometimes red) face*, and finely barred chest and belly. Imm. and juv. variably coloured brown and buff, with barred underwings and tail, and greyish-yellow bare facial skin. Large size, bare facial skin and long yellow legs distinguish it from other similarly plumaged raptors. **Status and habitat:** Common br. resident across woodland, savanna, suburbia and riparian forest. **SETSWANA: SE.GÔÔTSANE**

## Common Buzzard
*Buteo buteo*

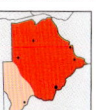

**45–52 cm** A medium-sized highly variably plumaged brown raptor with *lightly streaked upper chest, barred belly and flanks,* and yellow cere and legs. In flight, shows mostly dark brown upperwings, pale underwings, and lightly barred flight feathers with black tips and trailing edges. Juv. like ad., but heavily streaked and paler below, often with paler head. **Status and habitat:** Common non-br. summer migrant in most open habitats, including grassland, savanna and woodland. **SETSWANA: MMANKGÔDI**

## Pale Chanting Goshawk
*Melierax canorus*

**46–63 cm** *A large, tall grey goshawk with long red legs, red cere, white patches in secondaries* contrasting with black-tipped primaries, finely barred lower chest and belly, white rump and heavily banded tail. Juv. brown with banded tail, white rump and yellow-orange cere and legs. Ad. and juv. similar to Dark Chanting Goshawk. **Status and habitat:** A very common and familiar br. resident found in most open habitats, including semi-desert, arid savanna and tree-lined watercourses. **SETSWANA: SE.GÔÔTSANE**

## Dark Chanting Goshawk
*Melierax metabates*

**43–50 cm** A large, tall grey goshawk with *plain dark upperparts, heavily barred underparts, red cere and long, red legs.* Juv. mostly brown with orange-yellow legs and cere. Ad. very similar to slightly larger Pale Chanting Goshawk, but lacks pale wing bar; in flight, grey (not white) secondaries and grey (not white) rump apparent. Juv. separated from similar juv. Pale Chanting Goshawk by mottled-brown (not white) rump. **Status and habitat:** Uncommon resident in tall woodland, avoiding open habitats. **SETSWANA: SE.GÔÔTSANE**

## Gabar Goshawk — *Micronisus gabar*

**28–36 cm** A medium-sized grey goshawk with red legs and cere, white-tipped secondaries, white rump, heavily banded black-and-white tail, and heavily barred lower chest and belly. Uncommon black morph all black except for pale flight feathers and black-and-white banded tail. Juv. brown with streaked upper chest and barred lower chest and belly, and orange-red cere and legs. Ad. similar to Ovambo Sparrowhawk and Lizard Buzzard. **Status and habitat:** Common br. resident in savanna, and woodland.
SETSWANA: SE.GÔÔTSANE

## Ovambo Sparrowhawk
*Accipiter ovampensis*

**32–40 cm** A heavyset sparrowhawk with grey upperparts, *fine grey barring from vent to throat*, dark eyes, and orange-red cere and legs. In flight, shows barred underwings, dark rump and banded tail. Juv. has dark brown upperparts, white or pale rufous underparts, strong pale supercilium, and paler cere and legs. Ad. told from Gabar Goshawk by barred throat and upper chest, and from Shikra by eye, cere and leg colour.
**Status and habitat:** Uncommon resident in woodland. SETSWANA: NAME UNKNOWN

## Shikra — *Tachyspiza badia*

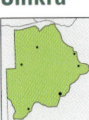

**28–30 cm** A medium-sized goshawk with *yellow cere and legs, bright red eyes*, light grey upperparts, rufous-and-white-barred belly, chest and throat, and banded tail with plain grey central feathers. Juv. brown above, with dark-blotched white underparts with faint black stripe on throat, orange-yellow cere and legs, and yellow eyes. Ad. distinguished from other medium-sized goshawks by coloration of bare parts.
**Status and habitat:** Uncommon br. resident found throughout Botswana in most wooded habitats. SETSWANA: NAME UNKNOWN

## Little Sparrowhawk *Tachyspiza minulla*

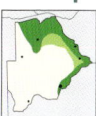

**23–27 cm** A *small sparrowhawk with yellow legs, cere, eyes and eye-ring,* grey upperparts and brown-barred white underparts. In flight, white rump and two white uppertail spots evident. Juv. brown above with dark streaks on throat and chest, with larger spots and blotches on belly and flanks. **Status and habitat:** Uncommon br. resident in tall woodland and other densely wooded habitats; often found in riparian vegetation. **SETSWANA: NAME UNKNOWN**

## Lizard Buzzard
*Kaupifalco monogrammicus*

**35–37 cm** A medium-sized hawk-like raptor with obvious *white throat with dark stripe,* plain grey upperparts and chest, finely barred belly, and red legs and cere. In flight, white rump and tail band evident. Similar to Gabar Goshawk, but has pale throat with dark stripe. **Status and habitat:** Uncommon resident in woodland and dense savanna. **SETSWANA: NAME UNKNOWN**

## Black-winged Kite *Elanus caeruleus*

**30–33 cm** A small kite with grey upperparts, *black shoulder patches and wing tips, white head and underparts,* red eyes, and yellow cere and legs. Juv. like ad., but with scaled upperparts and breast and rufous-washed nape. Regularly seen hovering while hunting for prey. **Status and habitat:** Uncommon br. resident across most open habitats throughout Botswana, including grassland, open savanna, agricultural land and semi-desert. **SETSWANA: PHAKALANE**

## Pygmy Falcon — *Polihierax semitorquatus*

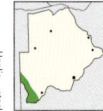

**18–20 cm** A tiny falcon with *grey upperparts, white underparts*, black-and-white-barred and -spotted flight feathers and tail, and orange-pink cere and legs. Female has chestnut back and mantle. *Strongly associated with Sociable Weaver (p. 124) nests, in which it breeds.* **Status and habitat:** Uncommon resident in semi-arid savanna and dry riverbeds in the extreme southwest.
**SETSWANA: NAME UNKNOWN**

## Rock Kestrel — *Falco rupicolus*

**30–34 cm** A slender, *mostly chestnut kestrel with grey head, indistinct dark moustachial stripe*, dark spots and streaks on upperparts, heavy dark streaks on paler underparts, finely barred grey tail, and yellow-orange cere and legs. Female lacks contrasting grey head. In flight, shows pale underwings with light barring. Similar to Greater Kestrel.
**Status and habitat:** Common resident across most open habitats, particularly in semi-arid areas. Mostly uses cliff faces to breed. **SETSWANA: PHAKALANE**

## Greater Kestrel — *Falco rupicoloides*

**33–38 cm** A fairly large, *round-headed, pale rufous kestrel* with heavily barred upperparts, lightly streaked underparts, and broadly barred grey tail. In flight, shows mostly plain white underwings with dark wing tips. Like Rock Kestrel, but lacks grey head and moustachial stripe, and has pale (not dark) eyes. **Status and habitat:** Common resident in open arid habitats, particularly in the Kalahari Desert. **SETSWANA: PHAKALANE**

## Dickinson's Kestrel — *Falco dickinsoni*

**28–30 cm** A medium-sized, *kestrel* with dark grey upperparts, *pale grey head, underparts and rump*, and *yellow cere, eye-ring*, and legs. Juv. with light brown wash and duller yellow or blue-green cere, eye-ring and legs. **Status and habitat:** Uncommon resident in savanna (favouring palm savanna) and open woodland. SETSWANA: **PHAKALANE**

## Red-necked Falcon — *Falco chicquera*

**30–36 cm** A medium-sized, distinctive-looking falcon, with obvious *rufous crown and nape*, distinct moustachial stripe, *heavily grey-barred upperparts* and pale-barred underparts. Juv. similar to ad., but with duller rufous head and nape, and indistinct brown patches on upper back. **Status and habitat:** Common to uncommon resident in open savanna, often with the presence of tall palm trees. SETSWANA: **NAME UNKNOWN**

## Lanner Falcon — *Falco biarmicus*

**36–48 cm** A large, powerful falcon with *rufous cap*, plain grey upperparts, and mostly *plain buff-white underparts*. Juv. with darker brown-grey upperparts, heavily streaked underparts and creamy (not rufous) cap. In flight, diffusely barred, long and broad wings, and long tail evident. Similar to smaller Eurasian Hobby (p. 42). Often seen hunting birds around desert waterholes. **Status and habitat:** Common widespread resident occurring in a range of habitats, including hilly areas, savanna, grassland and farmland. SETSWANA: **PHAKWE**

### Eurasian Hobby — *Falco subbuteo*

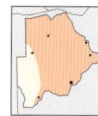

**28–36 cm** A small falcon with *heavily streaked underparts*, *contrasting plain white throat*, grey upperparts, *rufous vent*, *dark crown* with indistinct pale supercilium, and thin, pointed moustachial stripe. In flight, shows pointed wings, with heavily streaked and barred underwings, and all-grey upperwings. Juv. has creamier underparts and lacks rufous vent. All ages similar to larger juv. Lanner Falcon (p. 41), but with dark (not light brown) crown. **Status and habitat:** Uncommon non-br. summer migrant in most open habitats.
**SETSWANA: NAME UNKNOWN**

### Helmeted Guineafowl
*Numida meleagris*

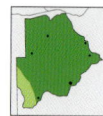

**55–60 cm** A large, highly recognisable game bird, with spotted body, small bare head with distinctive *bony casque and blue-and-red bare facial skin with wattles*. Juv. browner with partly feathered, striped head, lacking casque and wattles. Highly vocal and noisy, making a series of cackling sounds and a high-pitched breeding song.
**Status and habitat:** Common br. resident throughout its range. In most open habitats, from savanna to semi-desert.
**SETSWANA: KGAKA**

### Crested Francolin — *Ortygornis sephaena*

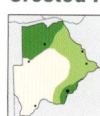

**30–35 cm** A small francolin with *clear white supercilium*, dark crown, and *tail often held cocked at 45° angle*. Neck and breast attractively marked with dark 'teardrops' and belly shows very faint barring. Upperparts heavily patterned with speckles (male) or barring (female). Small crest rarely observed and not a useful identification feature. **Status and habitat:** Common br. resident. Occurs in pairs and small coveys in thornveld and savanna, throughout the lusher north and east. **SETSWANA: LE.TSIËKWANE**

FRANCOLINS, SPURFOWL

## Coqui Francolin     *Campocolinus coqui*

**20–26 cm** A small francolin with *tawny-yellow head and heavily barred black-and-white underparts*, from lower neck to vent. Female markedly different, with black-bordered white throat, pale supercilium, tawny ear coverts, buffy chest, and less intensely barred underparts. **Status and habitat:** Uncommon resident of broadleaved woodland and savanna. SETSWANA: LE.TSIÊKWANE

## Orange River Francolin
*Scleroptila gutturalis*

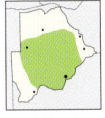

**32–35 cm** An attractively plumaged francolin with *black-bordered white or speckled throat, heavy chestnut streaks on breast and flanks*, and dark bill with yellow base to lower mandible. Lacks obvious white supercilium and cocked tail of Crested Francolin. **Status and habitat:** Common to uncommon br. resident, although absent from the northeast (including Okavango system), east and southwest. Occurs in Kalahari grassland and savanna. SETSWANA: KEDIKILÊ

## Red-billed Spurfowl
*Pternistis adspersus*

**35–38 cm** A mostly grey-brown spurfowl with finely barred body feathers (mostly on underparts), *yellow eye-ring*, red legs and *all-red bill*. Most similar to Natal Spurfowl (p. 44); superficially similar to Swainson's Spurfowl (p. 44), but has obvious yellow (not red) eye-ring, all-red (not black-and-red) bill, red (not black) legs and lack of bare red throat. **Status and habitat:** Common br. resident throughout most of Botswana where it is found in most wooded habitats. SETSWANA: LE.SOGO

SPURFOWLS, QUAIL

## Swainson's Spurfowl
*Pternistis swainsonii*

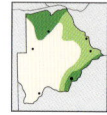

**33–38 cm** An all-brown spurfowl with *red eye-ring, bare red throat patch, black-and-red bill*, and dark legs. Given good views, easily separated from the superficially similar Red-billed Spurfowl (p. 43). **Status and habitat:** Common in grassland and savanna, across the northern and eastern parts of Botswana where it is a br. resident. Regularly occurs in transformed cultivation areas. **SETSWANA: KGWADI**

## Natal Spurfowl   *Pternistis natalensis*

**30–38 cm** A medium-sized spurfowl with heavily vermiculated brown upperparts, *intricately patterned black, white and grey underparts, red-tipped yellow bill* and red legs. Separated from similar Red-billed Spurfowl (p. 43) by red-and-yellow bill and lack of obvious yellow eye-ring. **Status and habitat:** Common localised resident in savanna, woodland and riparian forest. **SETSWANA: SE.GWÊBA**

## Harlequin Quail   *Coturnix delegorguei*

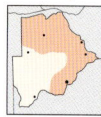

**14–18 cm** A strikingly patterned quail with *boldly patterned black-and-white face and throat*, pale-streaked dark brown upperparts, and *rufous and black underparts*. Female much duller, with buffy throat and supercilium, and lightly scaled rich buff underparts. Female superficially similar to Common Buttonquail, but has patterned face, dark eyes, and generally darker brown plumage. **Status and habitat:** Uncommon resident and intra-African br. summer migrant in open savanna and grassland. May be particularly numerous in wet years. **SETSWANA: SE.KHWIRI**

## Common Buttonquail — *Turnix sylvaticus*

**14–16 cm** Mostly seen when flushed, showing *dark flight feathers contrasting with dark-speckled light brown coverts*. Light brown, heavily speckled upperparts, buffy neck and scaled flanks evident if seen on ground. Female more brightly coloured, with brighter orange-buff on neck and throat. Female similar to female Harlequin Quail. **Status and habitat:** Common br. resident and nomad in grassland, agricultural land and open savanna. SETSWANA: **LE.PHURRWANA**

## Common Ostrich — *Struthio camelus*

**120–200 cm** An *unmistakable, massive flightless bird*. Male blackish, with white wings and tail, which is often stained brown. Female entirely grey-brown, sometimes very dark. Imm. resembles female, but smaller. Juv. sandy brown with spiky grey feathering on upperparts, and black dots and lines on neck. Male makes a deep booming '*hoo-hoo-hoooo*' call, like a lion's roar. **Status and habitat:** Common br. resident throughout most open habitats. SETSWANA: **MPSHE**

## Wattled Crane — *Grus carunculata*

**120–175 cm** *A massive crane with white neck, black belly, grey back and white-and-red wattles, bare red facial skin and grey crown*. Appears long-tailed due to elongated innermost wing feathers (tertials). Juv. paler than ad., with shortened tertial feathers, reduced white wattles and white crown and face. **Status and habitat:** Uncommon, yet conspicuous, br. resident on wetland edges and floodplains of the Okavango system. SETSWANA: **MO.GÔLÔDI**

ad.    juv.

### Kori Bustard
*Ardeotis kori*

**110–140 cm** Huge and distinctive-looking bustard; one of the heaviest flying birds in the world. *Barred grey neck, head crest and massive size* should differentiate it from any other regularly occurring bustards/korhaans. In display, male puffs up throat and erects crest and tail. **Status and habitat:** Common br. resident. Found in most open habitats including semi-desert of the Kalahari, grassland, open savanna and dry riverbeds. **SETSWANA: KGÔRI**

### Black-bellied Bustard
*Lissotis melanogaster*

**58–65 cm** A tall bustard with *black throat, foreneck, breast and belly, white cheeks*, and brown upperparts with dark chevrons. In flight, shows striking black-and-white patterning. Female dull brown below, with buff-grey neck and cheeks, and less white in wings. Similar to smaller Red-crested Korhaan, which lacks black line down foreneck and has mostly dark wings. **Status and habitat:** Uncommon resident in grassland and well-grassed savanna. **SETSWANA: MO.KGWÊBA**

### Red-crested Korhaan
*Lophotis ruficrista*

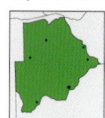

**48–50 cm** A relatively small bustard, with *intricate white chevrons on brown back*, black belly and grey or brown neck. Red crest of male rarely observed; only seen while displaying. Confusion likely with female Northern Black Korhaan, however, easily separated by the chevrons (not barring) on back. Superficially similar to Black-bellied Bustard. Utters a series of clicks, followed by high-pitched whistles, increasing in volume. **Status and habitat:** Common br. resident in most treed habitats, including savanna and woodland. **SETSWANA: MO.KGWÊBA**

## Northern Black Korhaan
*Afrotis afraoides*

**48–52 cm** Distinctly marked male unlikely to be confused with any other species; *black underparts and neck, white cheek patch, barred back, red bill and yellow legs*. Female much duller, similar to Red-crested Korhaan. Voice a loud, chaotic '*kewaak-kewaaak*' uttered from the ground or in display flight. **Status and habitat:** Common br. resident across open areas (grassland, open savanna and low vegetated dunes), avoiding denser woodland of north and east. **SETSWANA: TLATLAWÊ**

## Red-knobbed Coot     *Fulica cristata*

**36–44 cm** A large *grey-black waterbird with white bill and frontal shield, prominent red knobs on top of frontal shield,* and grey legs with lobed toes. Juv. mostly grey with dark bill and small dark frontal shield, lacking red knobs. Juv. similar to smaller juv. Common Moorhen (p. 48), which has pale flanks and undertail coverts, and dull olive legs. **Status and habitat:** Common resident in southeast, uncommon elsewhere. Found in most freshwater habitats, including dams, lakes and sewage works. **SETSWANA: KGOKGONOKA**

## African Swamphen
*Porphyrio madagascariensis*

**38–46 cm** A large, brightly plumaged waterbird with *green upperparts, purple-blue head and underparts, and large red bill, frontal shield and legs*. Regularly cocks tail, exposing bright white vent. Juv. paler and greyer than ad., with dusky red bill, frontal shield and legs. Ad. like smaller Allen's Gallinule (p. 48), but has red (not blue) frontal shield. Voice a series of loud honks and grunts. **Status and habitat:** Uncommon br. resident in well-vegetated wetlands and swamps, mostly restricted to the Okavango system. **SETSWANA: MMAMATHÊBÊ**

# GALLINULE, MOORHENS

### Allen's Gallinule — *Porphyrio alleni*

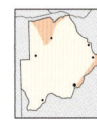

**25–28 cm** A medium-sized waterbird with *dark blue head, neck and underparts, green upperparts, red bill with blue* (greener in female) *frontal shield, and red legs*. Juv. mostly tan-brown with pale-scaled upperparts, dark bill and frontal shield, and flesh-coloured legs. Ad. like larger African Swamphen (p. 47); juv. like juv. Common Moorhen, but with scaled back and flesh-coloured (not olive-green) legs. **Status and habitat:** Uncommon intra-African br. summer migrant in well-vegetated wetlands, marshes and floodplains. SETSWANA: **MMAMATHÊBÊ**

### Common Moorhen — *Gallinula chloropus*

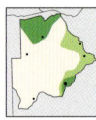

**30–38 cm** A mostly dark grey-black waterbird with obvious white flank stripes, *red-and-yellow bill with red frontal shield*, and bright yellow legs. Regularly cocks tail, exposing white undertail. Juv. grey-brown, with pale throat, and greenish-brown bill, frontal shield and legs. Ad. similar to Lesser Moorhen; juv. similar to juv. Allen's Gallinule, juv. Red-knobbed Coot (p. 47) and juv. Black Crake. **Status and habitat:** Common br. resident in well-vegetated wetlands, where it regularly feeds out in the open. SETSWANA: **KGOKGONOKA**

### Lesser Moorhen — *Paragallinula angulata*

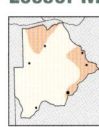

**22–26 cm** A small *pale grey* waterbird with *yellow bill with red ridge to upper mandible*. Juv. has light grey-brown upperparts, paler sandy brown underparts, and horn-coloured bill with dark base. All ages similar to larger Common Moorhen; ad. has much yellower bill, juv. has browner (not dark grey) plumage. **Status and habitat:** Uncommon intra-African br. summer migrant to freshwater habitats, including wetlands, floodplains and sewage works; may be particularly common in wet years. SETSWANA: **KGOKGONOKA**

## African Crake *Crecopsis egregia*

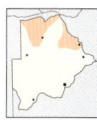

**19–23 cm** A mostly grey-and-brown crake with *heavily barred black-and-white lower breast and belly*, grey head and chest, dark-scalloped brown upperparts, and *red eyes, eye-ring, bill and legs*. Juv. darker and duller, with darker eyes, bill and legs. **Status and habitat:** Uncommon intra-African br. summer migrant to dry and flooded grassland and edges of seasonal wetlands; may be particularly abundant in wet years.
**SETSWANA: NAME UNKNOWN**

## Black Crake *Zapornia flavirostra*

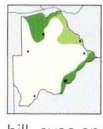

**18–23 cm** A small, *uniformly black crake with chrome yellow bill, and red eyes and legs*. Juv. dark grey-brown with paler throat, and dark bill, eyes and legs. Juv. similar to juv. Common Moorhen, but much smaller, lacks flank stripes and has dark (not olive-green) legs. Voice a loud, strange whinnying duet. **Status and habitat:** Common br. resident in well-vegetated wetlands. **SETSWANA: KOKWANA YANOKA**

## African Jacana *Actophilornis africanus*

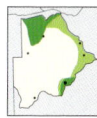

**25–32 cm** A distinctive-looking waterbird with *very large feet for walking on floating vegetation*. Plumage *mostly rich chestnut, with white neck and throat*, black eye-stripe running onto nape, and *blue frontal shield*. Juv. has white (not chestnut) underparts and dark crown with white supercilium (lacking blue frontal shield); may be confused with smaller Lesser Jacana (p. 50). **Status and habitat:** Common resident of the Okavango system, scattered and nomadic elsewhere, occurring in wetlands with floating vegetation (particularly water lilies).
**SETSWANA: MO.GATSA-KWÊNA**

### Lesser Jacana — *Microparra capensis*

**15–17 cm** Very similar to juv. African Jacana (p. 49), but told apart by *tiny size, lighter brown upperparts, buff-brown (not dark) crown and buff-orange neck sides.* In flight, white-tipped secondaries and paler upperwing coverts differ from the uniformly dark upperwing of juv. African Jacana. **Status and habitat:** Uncommon resident and nomad of the Okavango system and the extreme northeast. Occurs in both permanent and temporary wetlands and floodplains with a high level of cover from grasses and water lilies. SETSWANA: NAME UNKNOWN

### Spotted Thick-knee — *Burhinus capensis*

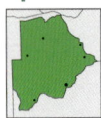

**43 cm** A large, mostly brown wader with heavily spotted upperparts, heavily streaked underparts, *large yellow eyes and long yellow legs.* Mostly seen roosting during the day time, but active at night. Voice a loud, frenetic, shrill whistle, heard mostly at night. **Status and habitat:** Common widespread resident of most open habitats, regularly found in sports fields and parks. SETSWANA: MO.NGWANGWA

### Water Thick-knee
*Burhinus vermiculatus*

**38–41 cm** Similar to Spotted Thick-knee, but smaller, with *obvious grey wing panel,* and streaked (not spotted) upperparts. Often seen during the day, roosting or partially active at water's edge. Voice a loud, mournful, descending whistle, mostly heard at night. **Status and habitat:** Common br. resident, strongly associated with freshwater aquatic habitats, including dams, floodplains, rivers and lakes. SETSWANA: LE.PHURRWANA

## Black-winged Stilt
*Himantopus himantopus*

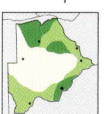

**35–40 cm** A tall wader with *long red legs, all-black wings, bright white head, neck and underparts, and long, straight bill.* Non-br. ad. shows dusky nape patch. Juv. similar, but with grey-black wings. **Status and habitat:** Common br. resident found in shallow wetlands and marshes, both permanent and ephemeral, as well as salt pans. SETSWANA: NAME UNKNOWN

## Pied Avocet
*Recurvirostra avosetta*

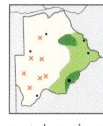

**42–45 cm** An unmistakable *black-and-white wader with strongly upturned thin black bill*, and long, grey legs. In flight, upperparts show black patches in wing tips, wing coverts and scapulars (where wing and body meet). Juv. like ad., but with mottled brown plumage. **Status and habitat:** Common br. resident and nomad. Mostly occurs in saline and temporary wetlands, including Makgadikgadi Pans. SETSWANA: NAME UNKNOWN

## Long-toed Lapwing
*Vanellus crassirostris*

**29–31 cm** A strikingly patterned lapwing with *white face, black breast band and nape,* brown back and white belly. In flight, shows mostly white wings with black outer wing, and white uppertail with broad black terminal bar. **Status and habitat:** Common br. resident restricted to the Okavango system in well-vegetated wetlands, floodplains and marshes. SETSWANA: THATSWANE WADIKUBU

## Blacksmith Lapwing  Vanellus armatus

**28–31 cm** A *black, white and grey lapwing* superficially resembling Long-toed Lapwing (p. 51), but with *mostly black head and neck, and white crown*. Juv. mottled and browner than ad. A highly vocal species, making a series of loud *'tink-tink-tink'* calls when alarmed, reminiscent of blacksmith hammering on anvil (hence common name). **Status and habitat:** A very common and conspicuous br. resident in any wetland habitat, as well as adjoining grasslands and floodplains. **SETSWANA: LE.THULATSHIPI**

## Crowned Lapwing  Vanellus coronatus

**29–31 cm** A mostly brown-and-white lapwing with *obvious black crown with white ring*, brown chest and back, white belly, faint black chest bar, and red bill base and legs. Juv. like ad., but with scaled upperparts, and duller red bill and legs. **Status and habitat:** Common and widespread br. resident in most open habitats, including grassland and scrub; also frequents playing fields and golf courses. **SETSWANA: LE.RWEERWEE**

## African Wattled Lapwing
*Vanellus senegallus*

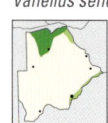

**34–35 cm** A large, mostly grey-brown lapwing with *obvious yellow facial wattles* with red base, *yellow legs* and bill, white forehead, streaked neck, and black bar on belly. Juv. like ad., but with reduced white crown and facial wattles. **Status and habitat:** Uncommon br. resident around the Okavango system and extreme southeast. Strongly tied to aquatic habitats, including wetland edges (and adjoining moist grasslands), marshes and exposed sandbanks in rivers. **SETSWANA: NAME UNKNOWN**

## Caspian Plover  *Anarhynchus asiaticus*

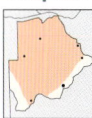

**18–22 cm** A medium-sized, long-legged plover with brown upperparts, broad *rufous breast band, white face, supercilium* and belly, longish thin bill, and *dull yellow legs*. Non-br. ad. has scalloped upperparts, *diffuse grey-brown breast band*, buffy face and supercilium, and *dark eye patch*. Juv. similar to smaller juv. Kittlitz's Plover, but lacks buffy nuchal collar and has dull yellow legs. **Status and habitat:** Uncommon Palearctic-br. summer migrant to poorly grassed open areas, fallow agricultural land and dry floodplains. **SETSWANA: NAME UNKNOWN**

## Common Ringed Plover
*Charadrius hiaticula*

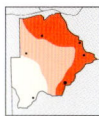

**18–20 cm** A small, boldly marked plover with obvious *black breast band, white nuchal collar, black-and-white forehead*, and orange legs and base of bill. Non-br. ad. and juv. with duller, reduced black breast band and forehead. **Status and habitat:** Common non-br. summer Palearctic migrant, strongly associated with aquatic habitats, from salt pans to marshes and wetland edges with exposed shoreline. **SETSWANA: NAME UNKNOWN**

## Chestnut-banded Plover
*Anarhynchus pallidus*

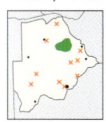

**15 cm** A small *pale plover* with light grey upperparts, obvious *chestnut breast band*, white face with black crown band and lores, and white underparts. Female has light chestnut crown band and lores. Juv. has incomplete grey breast band, and lacks patterning on head and face. **Status and habitat:** Common localised resident in salt pans of the Makgadikgadi Pans. **SETSWANA: NAME UNKNOWN**

### Three-banded Plover
*Charadrius tricollaris*

**18 cm** Easily recognisable plover with *three prominent breast bands* (two black and one white), *white crown ring, red bill base and eye-ring*, uniform dark brown back and wings and white belly. Juv. with less vivid black breast bands and crown ring, upperparts lightly scaled. **Status and habitat:** Common along the shorelines of most water bodies including wetlands, dams and sewage works. SETSWANA: THATSWANE

### Kittlitz's Plover   *Anarhynchus pecuarius*

**12–16 cm** A small plover with lightly scaled brown upperparts, buffy breast, brown crown with white ring, and *bold black eye-stripe extending across forehead, and nuchal collar around the back of the head*. Juv. has pale brown head pattern. Similar to non-br. Caspian Plover (p. 53). **Status and habitat:** Common br. resident found in short grassland, wetland edges, marshes and salt pans. SETSWANA: THATSWANE

### Greater Painted-Snipe
*Rostratula benghalensis*

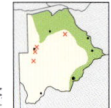

**23–26 cm** A *vividly marked and strongly sexually dimorphic wader with long, drooping bill,* and white eye-ring, eye-stripe and shoulder bar. Female more boldly marked, with chestnut head and throat, and brown, lightly barred upperparts. Male duller, with grey-brown head, golden and dark brown blotched upperparts and golden back 'braces'. **Status and habitat:** Uncommon resident and nomad. Prefers edges of shallow vegetated water bodies and marshes with exposed mud. SETSWANA: NAME UNKNOWN

SNIPE, RUFF, SANDPIPER

## African Snipe *Gallinago nigripennis*

**28–30 cm** A *long-billed wader* with dark-barred pale underparts, *intricately patterned brown upperparts*, dark crown stripe and eye-stripe, and pale supercilium. Most likely to be seen when flushed, uttering a sharp '*chuck*' and showing lightly barred white outer tail feathers. Uses stiff tail feathers during aerial display to produce bizarre roar, similar to sound of an aeroplane. **Status and habitat:** Common resident in well-vegetated wetlands, marshes, reed beds and floodplains. SETSWANA: NAME UNKNOWN

## Ruff *Calidris pugnax*

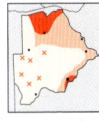

**20–30 cm** A medium-sized to large brown-and-white wader with *heavily scaled back and orange legs*, which differentiate it from other commonly occurring sandpipers; black bill often has orange base surrounded by white feathering. Male considerably larger than female. **Status and habitat:** Commonly occurring Palearctic-br. summer migrant. Occurs in most water bodies with exposed shoreline, and routinely feeds in adjoining flooded fields and floodplains. SETSWANA: NAME UNKNOWN

## Curlew Sandpiper *Calidris ferruginea*

**18–23 cm** *A medium-sized wader with long, drooping bill, longish black legs*, grey-brown upperparts, white underparts with light streaking on upper breast, and weak grey eye-stripe and supercilium. In flight, mostly white rump patch and thin pale wing bar evident. Similar to the smaller Little Stint (p. 56). **Status and habitat:** Common Palearctic-br. summer visitor to shorelines of any water body, including salt pans; often seen feeding in adjoining flooded fields with emergent vegetation.
SETSWANA: NAME UNKNOWN

### Little Stint — *Calidris minuta*

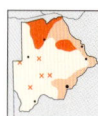

**12–15 cm** A small wader with uniform grey upperparts, white underparts with light streaking on upper breast, and medium-length black bill. In br. plumage (autumn and spring) grey upperparts replaced with rich brown scaling, breast and face infused with red-brown. Like Curlew Sandpiper (p. 55), but smaller, with shorter legs and shorter, mostly straight bill. **Status and habitat:** Commonly occurring Palearctic-br. summer migrant. Frequents exposed shorelines of water bodies, including salt pans and floodplains. SETSWANA: **NAME UNKNOWN**

### Common Sandpiper — *Actitis hypoleucos*

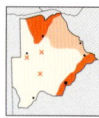

**19–21 cm** A dainty wader that *constantly bobs its tail*. Lightly barred brown upperparts, *obvious white shoulder crescents*, white underparts with dark smudging to upper breast, long tail, and medium-length straight bill. Lacks spotted upperparts and white rump of Wood Sandpiper. **Status and habitat:** Common Palearctic-br. summer migrant, regular at most water bodies, including quiet streams and sewage works. Solitary or in small groups, never occurs in large flocks. SETSWANA: **MO.SALAKATANE**

### Wood Sandpiper — *Tringa glareola*

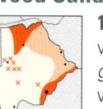

**19–21 cm** A medium-sized wader *with pale-spotted grey-brown upperparts*, white rump and belly, dusky breast and throat, dark eye-stripe, pale supercilium, medium-length straight bill and dull green legs. Similar to Common Sandpiper. **Status and habitat:** Common Palearctic-br. summer migrant to the shores of any water body, including sewage works, dams, marshes and floodplains. SETSWANA: **MO.SALAKATANE**

SANDPIPER, GREENSHANK, COURSER

## Marsh Sandpiper  *Tringa stagnatilis*

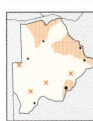

**22–26 cm** A medium-sized pale wader, *with long yellowish legs* and *straight, sharp-tipped all-black bill*; often shows grey-black shoulder patch. In flight, white rump and lower back form a white triangle. Similar to larger Common Greenshank, which has grey-based and slightly upturned bill and duller green-yellow legs. **Status and habitat:** Uncommon Palearctic-br. summer migrant, which may occur in any permanent or ephemeral wetland.
**SETSWANA: MO.SALAKATANE**

## Common Greenshank  *Tringa nebularia*

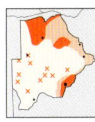

**30–34 cm** A large pale wader with *pale-based, slightly upturned bill and green-yellow legs*. A very active forager, which makes exaggerated side-to-side sweeps to find food. Voice a loud '*doop-doop-doop*' in flight, usually when disturbed. Similar to smaller Marsh Sandpiper sharing a white triangular-shaped patch to lower back and rump. **Status and habitat:** Common Palearctic-br. summer visitor, regular along shorelines of any water body. **SETSWANA: NAME UNKNOWN**

## Temminck's Courser
*Cursorius temminckii*

**19–21 cm** A small terrestrial wader with mostly brown plumage, *rufous crown, black and white stripes behind the eye,* dark belly patch, and white lower belly and vent. Unlikely to be confused with any regularly occurring coursers in Botswana. **Status and habitat:** Common to uncommon br. resident and nomad, found in most open habitats, including heavily grazed and short grassland, floodplains and burnt areas.
**SETSWANA: SE.GOLAGOLA**

### Double-banded Courser
*Rhinoptilus africanus*

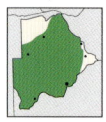

**20–25 cm** A pale courser with *two obvious black breast bands (wrapping around the neck) and heavily scaled upperparts*. Plain, pale face makes black eyes stand out. In flight, shows rufous wing patches and white rump. Easily overlooked due to habit of standing motionless in shade during heat of the day. Confusion with Temminck's Courser (p. 57) is unlikely. **Status and habitat:** Common br. resident, favouring open, sparsely vegetated or bare plains. **SETSWANA: SE.GOLAGOLA**

### Bronze-winged Courser
*Rhinoptilus chalcopterus*

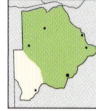

**25–28 cm** A large courser with *boldly marked face (black ear coverts and lores and white supercilium)*, brown upperparts and neck, white throat and belly, *single dark breast band*, red legs and red base to lower mandible. Nocturnally active; most likely to be seen in the day roosting in the shade of bushes. **Status and habitat:** Uncommon resident and local migrant in open savanna and woodland; numbers bolstered in summer. **SETSWANA: NAME UNKNOWN**

### Collared Pratincole *Glareola pratincola*

**24–25 cm** A tern-like mostly brown wader with *black-bordered, cream-yellow throat*. Most distinctive in flight, when *long deeply forked tail, white rump and mostly rufous underwings* obvious. Non-br. ad. lacks black border on throat. An aerial feeder, which flies with strong buoyant flight; may be seen in flocks of thousands. **Status and habitat:** Common br. resident, numbers increased in summer by intra-African migrants. Occurs on edges of wetlands and in open grassland areas near to water. **SETSWANA: LE.TLHAPÊLAPULA**

## Grey-headed Gull
*Chroicocephalus cirrocephalus*

**40–42 cm** The only commonly occurring gull in Botswana. Shows an *obvious light grey head, grey back, white underparts,* and red bill and legs. Non-br. ad. and juv. with much-reduced grey head, often restricted to dark smudges behind eye. **Status and habitat:** Uncommon br. resident found in wetland systems and salt pans. May also be seen at pans, dams and sewage works.
SETSWANA: NAME UNKNOWN

## African Skimmer  *Rynchops flavirostris*

**36–42 cm** A highly distinctive *black-and-white waterbird with long orange-red, yellow-tipped bill with noticeably longer lower mandible.* Feeds in characteristic manner, flying low and skimming water surface with lower mandible to find fish. Juv. shows slightly paler-fringed upperparts, with shorter, dark-tipped bill. **Status and habitat:** Locally common intra-African br. summer visitor to the Okavango system and extreme northeast, on exposed sandbanks of large rivers and lakes. SETSWANA: NAME UNKNOWN

## Whiskered Tern  *Chlidonias hybrida*

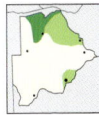

**23–26 cm** A lake tern with *dark grey underparts, slightly paler upperparts, white cheek, black cap,* and dull red bill and legs. Non-br. ad. and juv. with white underparts, mostly pale crown, and broad black eye-stripe extending beyond eye. Non-br. plumage like migrant White-winged Tern (p. 60), but paler above, with grey (not white) rump and head patterning, lacking black 'headphones'. **Status and habitat:** Common br. resident at wetlands, marshes, ephemeral pans, and large rivers. SETSWANA: NAME UNKNOWN

### White-winged Tern
*Chlidonias leucopterus*

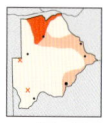

**20–22 cm** A small tern mostly seen in drab non-br. plumage, with white underparts, grey upperparts and darker mantle. *Black 'headphone' mark behind eye* separates it from similar Whiskered Tern (p. 59). Striking in br. plumage (rare in Botswana): black head and underparts, grey back, and white flight feathers contrasting with black underwing coverts. **Status and habitat:** Common to uncommon non-br. summer visitor, which frequents wetlands, marshes and sewage works. SETSWANA: NAME UNKNOWN

### Namaqua Sandgrouse
*Pterocles namaqua*

**24–28 cm** An intricately patterned sandgrouse with *long, pointed tail* (differentiating from other sandgrouse). Male has plain sandy brown face, neck and underparts, double breast band (white above, maroon below), and blue-grey-spotted upperparts. Female has streaked head and breast, barred belly and lacks breast band; can be confused with female Double-banded Sandgrouse. **Status and habitat:** Common br. nomad in arid and semi-arid plains. SETSWANA: LE.GWARAGWARA

### Double-banded Sandgrouse
*Pterocles bicinctus*

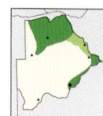

**25–26 cm** A buffy brown sandgrouse with dark brown upperparts with white spots and chestnut barring, and obvious yellow eye-ring. Male has *black-and-white bar on forehead and across the breast*. Female like female Namaqua Sandgrouse, but has barred (not streaked) chest and upper neck, and prominent yellow eye-ring. **Status and habitat:** Common br. resident in semi-arid woodland, savanna and dry riverbeds. SETSWANA: LE.GWARAGWARA

SANDGROUSE, DOVE, PIGEON     61

## Burchell's Sandgrouse
*Pterocles burchelli*

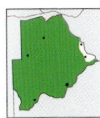

**24–26 cm** A *rich rufous sandgrouse with bold white spots above and below.* Male has grey face and throat with contrasting yellow eye-ring. Female has buffy yellow face and throat with subtle light grey eye-ring, and more heavily spotted and barred underparts. Separated from other sandgrouse by rich rufous plumage with white spots. **Status and habitat:** A widespread and common br. resident (and local nomad) in semi-arid savanna, favouring red Kalahari sands.
**SETSWANA: LE.GWARAGWARA**

♂

♀

## Rock Dove     *Columba livia*

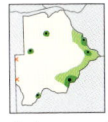

**32–34 cm** A large and *variably plumaged dove with glossy green-and-purple sheen to sides of neck.* Typical plumage includes darker grey head, pale grey underparts and upperparts, two broad wing bars and dark-tipped tail. Plumage can range from all dark to all white. **Status and habitat:** Common br. resident in large towns and cities with tall buildings. An introduced species, spreading across Botswana due to increased urban development.
**SETSWANA: LE.EBA**

## Speckled Pigeon     *Columba guinea*

**30–34 cm** A large pigeon with light grey head and underparts, *white-speckled maroon-brown upperparts,* maroon-orange neck with faint speckles and *bare red eye patch.* Paler grey lower back and rump evident in flight. **Status and habitat:** Common br. resident in naturally rocky areas, but has spread across much of the country, breeding in built-up areas and feeding in agricultural areas. **SETSWANA: LE.EBAROBA**

### Mourning Collared Dove
*Streptopelia decipiens*

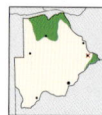

**28–30 cm** A large dove with brown-grey upperparts, pale grey head, *pinkish flush to chest, black hind collar, and pale yellow eyes contrasting with red eye-ring*. Similar to Red-eyed Dove, but smaller and paler with yellow (not dark red) eyes. Confusion also likely with Ring-necked Dove, which has dark eyes with pale eye-ring. **Status and habitat:** Common br. resident in woodland, particularly those surrounding the Okavango system. **SETSWANA: LE.EBA**

### Red-eyed Dove
*Streptopelia semitorquata*

**32–36 cm** A large dove with *purplish-grey upperparts*, paler pinkish-grey underparts, black hind collar, and *dark red eyes with red-purple eye-ring*. Confusion likely with Mourning Collared and Ring-necked doves, from which it differs by its larger size, darker coloration and buffy band on tail. Voice a deep hooting, rendered 'I-am-a-red-eyed-dove'. **Status and habitat:** Common br. resident in woodland, riparian forest and suburbia. **SETSWANA: LE.EBA**

### Ring-necked Dove *Streptopelia capicola*

**25–27 cm** A medium-sized dove with grey-brown upperparts, light to pink-grey underparts with white lower belly, *white-bordered black hind collar and jet black eyes (with thin, pale eye-ring)*. Similar to Mourning Collared and Red-eyed doves. Song is a high-pitched cooing, rendered 'work-HARDer'. **Status and habitat:** A very common br. resident, occurring in all wooded habitats, including savanna and suburbia. **SETSWANA: LE.PHÔI**

DOVES 63

## Laughing Dove — *Spilopelia senegalensis*

**22–25 cm** A smallish dove with pinkish-brown and blue-grey upperparts, *black-flecked rufous breast,* pale grey to white underparts and white-tipped outer tail. Lacks black hind collar or eye-ring. Voice a muffled '*hu-hu-HUU-hu-hu*'. **Status and habitat:** A very common br. resident, occurring in all wooded habitats, including savanna and suburbia, as well as agricultural areas.
SETSWANA: TSÔKWANE

## Emerald-spotted Wood Dove
*Turtur chalcospilos*

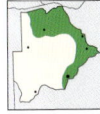

**17–20 cm** A small pinkish-brown dove with pale grey head and *iridescent green spots on upperwings. Bright rufous flight feathers* and two dark bands across lower back (visible only in flight). Voice a series of deep hoots, which speeds up and becomes higher pitched. **Status and habitat:** Common br. resident in dense woodland and savanna.
SETSWANA: MO.KUDUNYANE

## Namaqua Dove — *Oena capensis*

**24–28 cm** A small, *long-tailed dove* with iridescent purple spots in the upperwings and two black bands across lower back. Bright rufous flight feathers visible only in flight. Male has black face, throat and breast (lacking in female), and red-based yellow bill (all dark in female). Voice a deep '*huuuu-HUUUU*'.
**Status and habitat:** Common br. resident; nomadic in arid areas, in response to rainfall. Found in most wooded habitats and open arid to semi-arid savanna.
SETSWANA: RANKUDINYANE

### African Green Pigeon — *Treron calvus*

**25–30 cm** A *greenish-grey pigeon* with bright yellow leggings, red-and-white bill, pale eyes and dull purple shoulders. Voice a strange combination of whistles, growls and grunts. **Status and habitat:** Common br. resident in lush woodland and riparian forest, favouring areas with fruiting fig trees. **SETSWANA: LE.EBA**

### Meyer's Parrot — *Poicephalus meyeri*

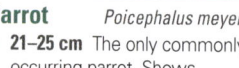

**21–25 cm** The only commonly occurring parrot. Shows mostly brown upperparts, *blue-green underparts, yellow shoulder patches* (most obvious in flight) and small yellow patch above eye. Juv. similar to ad., but lacks yellow markings. Voice a series of loud, typically parrot-like screeches and squawks. **Status and habitat:** A fairly common resident in woodland, including savanna and riparian forest. **SETSWANA: HÊGHA**

### Grey Go-away-bird — *Crinifer concolor*

**48–50 cm** A medium-sized, *all-grey turaco with long tail and pointed crest*; unlikely to be confused with any other species. Call is diagnostic, a loud nasal '*kweeeee*', or '*g'waaay*', hence the onomatopoeic common name. **Status and habitat:** Common br. resident in savanna, woodland and well-wooded gardens. **SETSWANA: MO.KOE**

## Great Spotted Cuckoo
*Clamator glandarius*

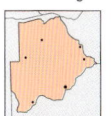

**37–42 cm** *A large long-tailed cuckoo with heavily spotted upperparts and cream-coloured to white underparts.* Head light grey with small crest. Juv. similar to ad. but head black and flight feathers chestnut (grey-olive in ad.). Voice a loud, almost raptor-like, '*kreaah-kreeah*' with frantic chattering. Brood parasite of crows and starlings. **Status and habitat:** Common br. intra-African summer visitor, widespread in woodland and open savanna. SETSWANA: **NAME UNKNOWN**

juv.
ad.

## Levaillant's Cuckoo
*Clamator levaillantii*

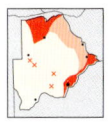

**38–40 cm** *A large black-and-white cuckoo with streaked throat and breast, and distinctive crest.* White wing and tail patches evident in flight. Resembles Jacobin Cuckoo, however, larger, with heavily streaked (not plain) underparts. Voice a trilling '*kreeu-kreeu-kreeu*' followed by chattering. Brood parasite of babblers. **Status and habitat:** A fairly common intra-African br. summer migrant that occurs in open savanna and woodland. SETSWANA: **MO.RÔKAPULA**

## Jacobin Cuckoo    *Clamator jacobinus*

**34 cm** Very similar to Levaillant's Cuckoo, however, *smaller and lacks streaking on underparts.* Occurs in two colour morphs: a black-and-white morph and a dark morph, which has all-black plumage except for white patches in wing. Voice very similar to Levaillant's Cuckoo and includes trills and chattering. Brood parasite of bulbuls and Southern Fiscal (p. 89). **Status and habitat:** Common intra-African br. summer migrant that occurs in woodland and open savanna. SETSWANA: **NÔNYANE**

black-and-white morph
dark morph

### Black Cuckoo — *Cuculus clamosus*

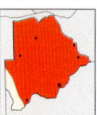

**28–31 cm** A medium-sized, *mostly glossy black cuckoo*, occasionally with faint rufous-barred underparts. Underwing distinctly barred grey. Female often more heavily barred below. Song a mournful whistled '*hoo-hoo-heeee*', rising in pitch and rendered '*I'm so siiiick*'. May be confused with black morph Jacobin Cuckoo (p. 65), but lacks white wing patches and crest. Brood parasite of boubous and Crimson-breasted Shrike (p. 87). **Status and habitat:** Common intra-African br. summer migrant found in open and dense woodland. **SETSWANA: MAKOKWE**

### African Cuckoo — *Cuculus gularis*

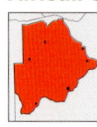

**30–33 cm** A *medium-sized, grey-and-white cuckoo with heavily barred underparts, and orange-yellow eye-ring and bill base.* Juv. darker grey above with pale tips to upperparts. Unlikely to be confused with any other commonly occurring cuckoo in Botswana. Song is a plaintive '*hoop-hoop*', similar to that of African Hoopoe (p. 74). Brood parasite of Fork-tailed Drongo (p. 91). **Status and habitat:** Widespread and fairly common intra-African br. summer migrant that occurs in savanna and woodland. **SETSWANA: NAME UNKNOWN**

### Diederik Cuckoo — *Chrysococcyx caprius*

**17–20 cm** A small green-and-white cuckoo, with white patches in wing, supercilium and lores, *and red eyes and eye-ring*. Female browner, with faint eye-ring. Juv. mostly brown above, with speckled underparts, red bill, and lacks eye-ring. Klaas's Cuckoo is similar, but has all-green wings and lores and white outer tail. Name is onomatopoeic for its whistled '*dee-dee-deederik*' song. Brood parasite of weavers, bishops and sparrows. **Status and habitat:** A very common intra-African br. summer visitor that occurs in wooded areas. **SETSWANA: NAME UNKNOWN**

## Klaas's Cuckoo  *Chrysococcyx klaas*

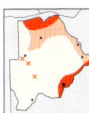

**16–18 cm** A small green-and-white cuckoo; similar to Diederik Cuckoo. Male *all-green above* and white below, with white patch behind eye and *pale eye-ring*. Female has barred green-and-brown upperparts, moderately barred underparts, brown head, and lacks eye-ring. Juv. like female but more heavily barred. Voice a clear, whistled '*may-kee*'. Brood parasite of batises, warblers and sunbirds. **Status and habitat:** Mostly common intra-African br. summer visitor in woodland, savanna and suburbia.
**SETSWANA: NAME UNKNOWN**

## Senegal Coucal  *Centropus senegalensis*

**38–40 cm** A medium-sized coucal with *black head and nape, white underparts, chestnut wings and black tail*. Very similar to larger Coppery-tailed Coucal, but shows rich rufous mantle, entirely unbarred rump and uppertail, and lacks glossy sheen to black head. Makes deep, bubbling descending notes. **Status and habitat:** Common to uncommon br. resident around Okavango system and other damp areas. Found on edges of woodland and grassland, in areas of thick scrub. **SETSWANA: LE.FUTUTU**

## Coppery-tailed Coucal
*Centropus cupreicaudus*

**46–52 cm** A very large coucal with typical coucal coloration, but shows a *dark or dirty brown mantle*, with *glossy violet sheen to black head, nape and tail; rump and uppertail heavily barred*. Makes deep, bubbling descending notes. **Status and habitat:** Common resident in swamps, marshes and reed beds (particularly favouring papyrus) of the Okavango system and other wetland areas. Strongly associated with wetland habitats, more so than any other coucal. **SETSWANA: LE.FUTUTU**

### White-browed Coucal
*Centropus superciliosus*

**40–41 cm** A medium-sized coucal separated from other coucals by *prominent white supercilium*, and *white streaks* on nape, mantle and dirty brown underparts. Rump and tail coverts are heavily barred (unlike Senegal Coucal, p. 67). Makes deep, bubbling descending notes. **Status and habitat:** Common br. resident in reed beds, rank grass, thickets and woodland edges, usually near water. **SETSWANA: LE.FUTUTU**

### Black Coucal                     *Centropus grillii*

**35–38 cm** A distinctive coucal with *black head and underparts, and heavily barred rufous wings*. Non-br. ad. and juv. have dark brown upperparts with rufous barring, and light brown underparts with white streaks; similar to other juv. coucals, but with heavier streaking and barring. Makes a clear '*pop-pop*' call. **Status and habitat:** Uncommon intra-African br. summer migrant occurring in rank grassland.
**SETSWANA: NAME UNKNOWN**

### Western Barn Owl                  *Tyto alba*

**30–35 cm** A medium-sized, *ghostly pale owl* with golden-brown-and-grey upperparts, white spotted underparts, heart-shaped pale facial disc, dark eyes, and pale grey-brown legs and feet. Voice a *loud, high-pitched eerie screech*. **Status and habitat:** Common and widespread resident found in most open habitats, including savanna, grassland, agricultural areas and even semi-desert. **SETSWANA: SE.KEA**

## Pearl-spotted Owlet
*Glaucidium perlatum*

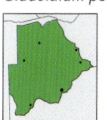

**17–21 cm** A small brown owl with *white spots on forehead* and upperparts, *black 'false eyes' on back of head*, pale underparts with dark streaks, and bright yellow eyes. Voice a series of high-pitched descending whistles. Similar to African Barred Owlet, which lacks 'false eyes', but upperparts and upper breast spotted (not barred), and lower breast and belly heavily streaked (not blotched). **Status and habitat:** Common br. resident in savanna and woodland. SETSWANA: MMANKGÔTLHWĚ

## African Barred Owlet
*Glaucidium capense*

**20–22 cm** A small owl with lightly barred brown upperparts, broadly barred tail, white scapular bar, white underparts with *barring on upper chest, and triangular blotches on belly*, and bright yellow eyes. Voice a series of whinnying whistles. Similar to Pearl-spotted Owlet. **Status and habitat:** Common br. resident in tall woodland and riparian forest. SETSWANA: MO.RUBISANA

## African Scops Owl  *Otus senegalensis*

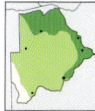

**14–18 cm** A *tiny grey owl* with dark streaks and vermiculations, lightly barred wings, *pointed 'ear' tufts*, black-bordered grey facial disc, and bright yellow eyes. Similar in size to Pearl-spotted and African Barred owlets; separated by presence of 'ear' tufts and mostly grey plumage. Voice a soft, yet far-carrying, '*prrrrrp*', repeated for long periods. **Status and habitat:** Common br. resident in savanna and tall woodland.
SETSWANA: SE.KOPAMARUMO

### Southern White-faced Owl
*Ptilopsis granti*

**25–28 cm** A medium-sized, mostly grey owl with dark vermiculations, *prominent, black-bordered white facial disc,* tall 'ear' tufts, orange-red eyes and grey bill. Voice a hooted '*hu-hu-hu-hu-HUUUUU*', with emphasis on the final note. **Status and habitat:** Common widespread br. resident in savanna, woodland and riparian vegetation.
**SETSWANA: KUKURUMA**

### Marsh Owl
*Asio capensis*

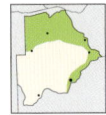

**35–38 cm** A medium-sized owl with plain brown upperparts, *cinnamon-brown underparts,* and light *grey, clearly demarcated facial disc.* In flight, shows barred flight feathers with paler underwings and dark 'comma' mark at base of primaries. **Status and habitat:** Uncommon resident and nomad in open habitats, including marshes, grassland and shrubland. **SETSWANA: MO.RUBISE**

### Spotted Eagle-Owl
*Bubo africanus*

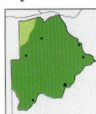

**43–50 cm** A *large, grey-brown owl* with heavily spotted upperparts, darkly spotted and barred underparts, *prominent 'ear' tufts,* black-bordered pale facial disc, and bright yellow eyes. Voice a deep hooted '*HUUUUU-huuuu*', with emphasis on the first note. **Status and habitat:** Common br. resident in a variety of habitats, including savanna, woodland, rocky outcrops, suburbia and semi-desert.
**SETSWANA: MMANKGÔTLHÔ**

## Verreaux's Eagle-Owl  *Ketupa lactea*

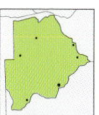

**58–66 cm** *A huge owl* with grey-brown upperparts, white shoulder bar, finely barred and scaled underparts, *black-bordered pale facial disc,* dark eyes, pink eyelids, and short 'ear' tufts. Voice a deep, far-carrying grunt. **Status and habitat:** Uncommon br. resident in low densities in savanna, woodland and riparian forest. SETSWANA: **MMANKGÔTLHÔ**

## Pel's Fishing Owl  *Scotopelia peli*

**60–64 cm** *A huge ginger-coloured owl,* with faint black barring on upperparts, dark streaks on chest, chevrons on belly, and large jet-black eyes; lacks 'ear' tufts. Voice a deep, far-carrying booming 'hoooooommmm-hu'. **Status and habitat:** Uncommon to rare br. resident, *strongly associated with aquatic habitats,* restricted to swamps and riparian forest of the Okavango system, with large overhanging trees from which it fishes at night. SETSWANA: **NQUMU**

## Rufous-cheeked Nightjar
*Caprimulgus rufigena*

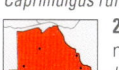

**22–24 cm** Pale grey-brown nightjar, *with buff-orange hind collar and small white patch in outer tail feathers and primaries.* Female has buff patches in tail and primaries. Like Fiery-necked Nightjar (p. 72), but has paler orange hind collar, reduced white in tail and all-dark rictal bristles. Nightjars are best differentiated by call; Rufous-cheeked makes loud, prolonged consistent churring, unlike Square-tailed Nightjar (p. 72). **Status and habitat:** Common br. summer visitor in most open woodland; frequently around waterholes. SETSWANA: **LE.TSÔBU**

### Fiery-necked Nightjar
*Caprimulgus pectoralis*

**23–25 cm** A dark grey-brown nightjar, with a *rich chestnut hind collar, large white outer tail patches and highly distinctive song*. Very similar to Rufous-cheeked (p. 71) and Square-tailed nightjars. Viewed up close, pale-based rictal bristles differentiate it from other nightjar species. Song is a whistled '*tuu-whit-tu-wuwuwu*', the final note being a trill. **Status and habitat:** Common br. resident in lush woodland and woodland edge. SETSWANA: MMAMPHUPHAMA

### Square-tailed Nightjar
*Caprimulgus fossii*

**22–25 cm** A light brown nightjar, with *entirely white outer tail feathers and bold white bars on folded wing*. Female has buff in wing and outer tail. Separated from Rufous-cheeked (p. 71) and Fiery-necked nightjars by all-white (or buff) outer tail feathers and broad white (or buff) bars in folded wing; and by churring call, which changes speed and pitch. **Status and habitat:** Common br. resident. Prefers moist open-country and woodland edges; regularly occurs in floodplains. SETSWANA: MMAMPHUPHAMA

### African Palm Swift   *Cypsiurus parvus*

**15–16 cm** A small *grey-brown swift with long, slender wings and long, deeply forked tail*. Most likely to be confused with Common Swift, but much lighter grey, with more delicate structure, more slender wings and longer, more deeply forked tail. **Status and habitat:** Common br. resident in savanna; range is linked to the presence of palm trees, within which it breeds. Occurs in towns where palms have been planted. SETSWANA: PÊOLANE

SWIFTS 73

### Common Swift   *Apus apus*

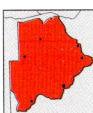

**17–18 cm** A large, *powerfully built and uniformly blackish-brown swift*, which may appear all-black at a distance. White throat patch and lightly scaled underparts only evident if seen well. Superficially resembles African Palm Swift. **Status and habitat:** Common non-br. summer visitor. Entirely aerial; often in huge flocks when avoiding rainy conditions or approaching storms. SETSWANA: **PÊOLANE**

### White-rumped Swift   *Apus caffer*

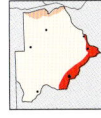

**14–16 cm** A slim, dark swift with *thinnish white rump*, pale throat, and *deeply forked tail*. Superficially similar to Little Swift, but easily separated by deeply forked (not square-ended) tail and much slimmer build. **Status and habitat:** Common localised intra-African br. summer migrant occurring in most open habitats. SETSWANA: **PÊOLANE**

### Little Swift   *Apus affinis*

**12–13 cm** A small, stocky black swift, with *obvious white rump and square-ended tail*; this *combination* makes confusion with other swifts unlikely. Viewed up close, the white throat is evident. Flocks often emit high-pitched shrill screams. Similar to slimmer White-rumped Swift. **Status and habitat:** Common br. resident, with numbers bolstered in summer by migrant populations. Breeds in steep rocky areas and built-up areas, such as the eaves of buildings and bridges, however, forages over most habitat types. SETSWANA: **PÊOLANE**

### Red-faced Mousebird
*Urocolius indicus*

**32–34 cm** The only widespread and common mousebird in Botswana. *Shows grey plumage, long tail, bare red facial mask,* black bill with red base, and pinkish-red legs. Juv. like ad. but facial mask greenish. A highly vocal species; voice a musical whistled '*chi-vu-vu*'. **Status and habitat:** Common resident in savanna, woodland and suburbia. **SETSWANA: LE.TSIABABA**

### African Hoopoe
*Upupa africana*

**25–28 cm** A distinctively shaped and plumaged bird; mostly *rufous with bold black-and-white-striped wings, obvious long crest and long, thin decurved bill.* Sexes differ slightly in black-and-white wing patterning. Juv. duller buff below, with buff in wings and shorter crest. Crest fanned when alarmed. Voice a quiet, but far-carrying, '*hoo-hoo*', from which onomatopoeic name is derived. **Status and habitat:** Common resident in woodland, savanna and suburbia. **SETSWANA: MMADILÊPÊ**

### Green Wood Hoopoe
*Phoeniculus purpureus*

**32–36 cm** A large, *iridescent green-and-purple wood hoopoe with long, white-tipped tail, and long, decurved red bill.* In flight, shows obvious white wing bars. Juv. like ad., but duller, with dark bill. Voice a loud cackling, made by territorial groups. Similar to Common Scimitarbill, but told apart by less decurved, red bill, mostly green plumage and red legs; juv. separated by shorter, straighter bill. **Status and habitat:** Common to uncommon resident in woodland, riparian forest and suburbia. **SETSWANA: LE.TSHÊGA-NÔGA**

## Common Scimitarbill
*Rhinopomastus cyanomelas*

**24–28 cm** A small wood hoopoe with mostly *dark iridescent blue-and-purple plumage, strongly decurved black bill,* and long tail with white spots on outer feathers. In flight, shows obvious white wing bars. Juv. like ad., but duller with shorter bill. Voice a sombre, deep-whistled '*weep-weep-weep*'. Similar to Green Wood Hoopoe but has more decurved, black bill and lacks green plumage. **Status and habitat:** Common resident in savanna and woodland. SETSWANA: SEBÔDU

## Southern Ground Hornbill
*Bucorvus leadbeateri*

**90–130 cm** An *unmistakable, massive terrestrial hornbill with black plumage, and bare red facial skin and neck pouch*. In flight, shows large white patch to wing tips. Juv. similar to ad., but facial skin cream coloured. Voice a very deep and far-carrying boom. **Status and habitat:** Uncommon resident of open broadleaved woodland. SETSWANA: LE.HUTUTU

## Southern Red-billed Hornbill
*Tockus rufirostris*

**35–45 cm** A small *black-and-white hornbill with red bill,* white spots on dark coverts, white underparts with grey streaking and smudging, and pale eyes. In flight, shows white on inner upperwings and outer tips of tail. Juv. with dark eyes and orange bill. Voice a series of high clucking notes. Confusion possible with Bradfield's Hornbill (p. 76), which is larger, with brown plumage, and orange bill. **Status and habitat:** Common resident of open woodland and savanna. SETSWANA: KÔRWÈ

### Southern Yellow-billed Hornbill
*Tockus leucomelas*

**48–60 cm** A medium-sized *black-and-white hornbill with large, bright yellow bill*, white spots on dark coverts, white underparts with slight grey streaking and smudging on neck and face, and pale eyes. In flight, shows white on inner upperwings and outer tips of tail. Juv. similar to ad., but plumage slightly dusky. Voice a series of high clucking notes. **Status and habitat:** A very common resident of open savanna and woodland. SETSWANA: KÔRWÊ

### Bradfield's Hornbill
*Lophoceros bradfieldi*

**50–57 cm** A medium-sized *mostly grey-brown hornbill with all-orange bill*, light scaling on upperparts, white belly, lower chest and outer tail tips, and pale orange eyes. Voice a series of loud, high-pitched whistling calls, which rise and drop in pitch. Confusion possible with smaller Southern Red-billed Hornbill (p. 75), which has black-and-white plumage and red bill. **Status and habitat:** Common to uncommon resident in woodland. SETSWANA: KÔRWÊ

### African Grey Hornbill
*Lophoceros nasutus*

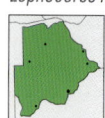

**44–50 cm** A small to medium-sized, *mostly grey hornbill with creamy supercilium*, black eyes. Bill black with creamy flash at base (male) or creamy with black base to lower mandible and red tip (female). In flight, shows white lower back and tips to grey tail. Voice a high-pitched plaintive whistle. **Status and habitat:** Common resident of open savanna and woodland. SETSWANA: KÔRWÊ

## Purple Roller  *Coracias naevius*

**35–40 cm** *A large, heavyset roller with olive upperparts, broad white supercilium, and pale-streaked lilac underparts.* In flight, shows shortish, square-ended tail and bright purple-blue flight feathers, striking in flight. Similar to Lilac-breasted Roller, but larger, lacking light blue coloration and long tail with streamers. **Status and habitat:** Common to uncommon resident in open savanna and woodland. SETSWANA: **LE.TLÊRÊTLÊRÊ**

## Lilac-breasted Roller
*Coracias caudatus*

**28 cm** A medium-sized, *long-tailed roller with pale lilac breast and throat*, brown upperparts, green nape, light blue belly, white chin and supercilium. In flight, shows bright blue, elongated outer tail feathers, and striking pale blue coverts contrasting with dark flight feathers. Similar to Purple Roller and European Roller. **Status and habitat:** Common resident in savanna and riparian woodland. SETSWANA: **LE.TLÊRÊTLÊRÊ**

## European Roller  *Coracias garrulus*

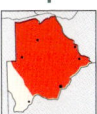

**30–32 cm** A heavyset roller with *light blue head and underparts*, and mostly brown upperparts with light blue shoulder patch. In flight, light blue coverts contrast with dark flight feathers. Similar to Lilac-breasted Roller, but plumage mostly light blue (lacking lilac breast) and tail short (lacking tail streamers). **Status and habitat:** Common non-br. summer visitor occurring in open savanna. SETSWANA: **LE.TLÊRÊTLÊRÊ**

# ROLLER, KINGFISHERS

## Broad-billed Roller
*Eurystomus glaucurus*

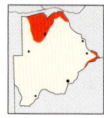

**27–29 cm** A colourful *yellow-billed roller* with *purple throat, breast and belly*, cinnamon crown, back and upperwing coverts, dark blue upperwing flight feathers and pale blue vent. In flight, shows pale blue underwing feathers and shallowly forked tail, with dark, inverted 'T' evident when spread. Voice a series of loud and harsh squawks and cackles. **Status and habitat:** Localised and common intra-African br. summer migrant in tall moist woodland and riparian forest. **SETSWANA: LE.TLÊRÊTLÊRÊ**

## Giant Kingfisher     *Megaceryle maxima*

**40–45 cm** A large, highly distinctive kingfisher with *white-spotted and -streaked black upperparts and head*, shaggy crest, *rufous chest*, speckled belly and *heavy black bill*. Female has *rufous belly* and speckled chest. **Status and habitat:** Uncommon to common localised resident in aquatic habitats, including rivers, lakes and small ponds. **SETSWANA: SE.INWÊDI**

## Pied Kingfisher     *Ceryle rudis*

**23–25 cm** A highly distinctive *black-and-white kingfisher* with *double breast band*, small crest and longish black bill. Female has *single incomplete breast band*. Regularly seen hovering when fishing. **Status and habitat:** Common resident in most aquatic habitats, including rivers, wetlands, lakes, dams and ponds. **SETSWANA: SE.INWÊDI**

## Malachite Kingfisher
*Corythornis cristatus*

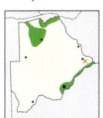

**14 cm** A small brightly coloured kingfisher with *bright blue upperparts, rufous-orange underparts*, black-barred blue-green crown, white throat and nape patch and *bright red bill*. Juv. has black bill. When excited, raises crown feathers as a crest. **Status and habitat:** Common resident in well-vegetated aquatic habitats, including rivers, streams, wetlands, dams and ponds. **SETSWANA: SE.INWÊDI**

## Striped Kingfisher    *Halcyon chelicuti*

**16–19 cm** A small, non-aquatic kingfisher with *lightly streaked crown and underparts, thick black eye-stripe extending onto nape, pale collar,* bicoloured bill (black upper mandible, red lower mandible), grey-black mantle and shoulders, and light blue lower back, tail and secondaries. Superficially similar to larger Woodland Kingfisher, but differs in upperpart coloration and crown pattern. **Status and habitat:** Common resident in savanna and woodland. **SETSWANA: SE.INWÊDI**

## Woodland Kingfisher
*Halcyon senegalensis*

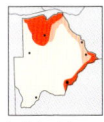

**22–24 cm** A medium-sized, *mostly blue-and-white* kingfisher with *bicoloured bill (red upper mandible, black lower mandible),* bright blue upperparts with black shoulder patches, grey-white underparts, and dark eye-stripe extending just beyond eye. Voice a loud '*chep-churrrrr*' with emphasis on the final trilling note. Similar to smaller Striped Kingfisher. **Status and habitat:** Common br. summer visitor in savanna and woodland. **SETSWANA: SE.INWÊDI**

## Swallow-tailed Bee-eater
*Merops hirundineus*

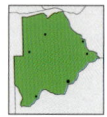

**20–22 cm** A small, *mostly green bee-eater* with thick black eye-stripe, yellow throat with blue collar, light blue lower belly and *deeply forked tail*. In flight, shows rufous primaries and secondaries with black subterminal band. Juv. like ad., but duller. Similar to Little Bee-eater which has black collar, orange underparts and shallowly forked tail. **Status and habitat:** Common resident and local nomad in savanna and semi-desert scrub; often found in well-vegetated dry riverbeds in Kalahari. **SETSWANA: SE.SÊLAMARUMÔ**

## Little Bee-eater
*Merops pusillus*

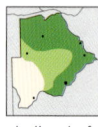

**15–17 cm** A very small bee-eater with *green upperparts, orange underparts*, thick black eye-stripe, yellow throat with black collar, and shallowly forked, rufous-and-black tail. Similar to Swallow-tailed Bee-eater, which has blue collar, blue-green underparts and deeply forked tail. Juv. like ad., but duller and lacks black collar. **Status and habitat:** Common resident in savanna and open bushy areas. **SETSWANA: SE.SÊLAMARUMÔ**

## White-fronted Bee-eater
*Merops bullockoides*

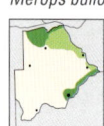

**22–24 cm** A medium-sized, *colourful bee-eater* with green upperparts, cinnamon underparts and head, thick black eye-stripe, white frons, white-and-red throat, bright blue rump and vent, *and square-ended tail* (lacking tail streamers). **Status and habitat:** Common resident in woodland and bushy areas near water bodies with sandy banks to nest in.
**SETSWANA: SE.SÊLAMARUMÔ**

## Blue-cheeked Bee-eater
*Merops persicus*

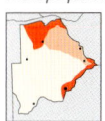

**24–26 cm** A medium-sized, *mostly green bee-eater* with blue-green head, light blue underparts, blue-edged black eye-stripe, yellow-and-rufous chin, and *elongated central tail streamers*. Worn ad. with much paler duller green plumage. **Status and habitat:** Common Palearctic-br. summer visitor to lake shores, floodplains and associated woodland; seldom far from water. SETSWANA: MORÔKAPULA

## European Bee-eater  *Merops apiaster*

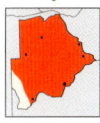

**25–29 cm** A medium-sized to large, colourful bee-eater with *blue underparts, yellow throat, black collar, golden back*, chestnut crown and nape, whitish frons, black eye-stripe, *and elongated central tail feathers*. Juv. like ad., but duller. **Status and habitat:** Common, widespread Palearctic-br. summer visitor in savanna and woodland. SETSWANA: MORÔKAPULA

## Southern Carmine Bee-eater
*Merops nubicoides*

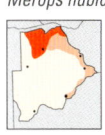

**24–27 cm** A *large, mostly pink-red bee-eater* with turquoise crown, rump, lower belly and vent, and *very long elongated central tail feathers*. Juv. like ad., but duller with shortened tail streamers. **Status and habitat:** Common br. summer visitor in savanna, woodland and floodplains with nearby water bodies. Mostly breeds in sandbanks along rivers. SETSWANA: MORÔKAPULA

### Acacia Pied Barbet
*Tricholaema leucomelas*

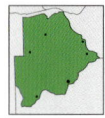

**17–18 cm** A *black-and-white barbet* with yellow-spotted black upperparts, *boldly striped head with red forehead spot*, white underparts with black throat, and heavy black bill. In flight, shows yellow lower back and rump. Voice a nasal '*neh*' and deep '*oooop*', both repeated multiple times. **Status and habitat:** Common resident in savanna and arid woodland.
SETSWANA: TLHÔLABAÊNG

### Black-collared Barbet
*Lybius torquatus*

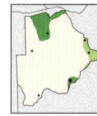

**19–20 cm** A large barbet with black head and collar, *red face and throat*, brown upperparts with golden-yellow edging to primaries, yellowish-white lower breast and belly, and heavy black bill. Voice a repeated '*tooo-puuudly*', sung as a duet. **Status and habitat:** Common resident in woodland, moist savanna and suburbia. SETSWANA: KOPAOPÊ

### Crested Barbet   *Trachyphonus vaillantii*

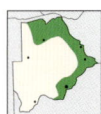

**24 cm** A large, mostly *yellow-and-black barbet with a black crest*, yellow face and head with red speckles, black upperparts with pale feather edges, yellow rump, red uppertail, yellow-orange underparts, and lightly spotted black breast band. Voice a loud and prolonged trilled '*trrrrrr*'. **Status and habitat:** Common resident in moist woodland, savanna, riparian forest and suburbia. SETSWANA: KÔKÔPA

## HONEYGUIDE, WOODPECKERS

### Greater Honeyguide *Indicator indicator*

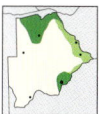

**18–20 cm** A large honeyguide with *boldly marked face with pale ear patches, black throat, pink bill,* brownish upperparts with pale edges to wing coverts and outer tail, and pale underparts. Female has plain face and dark bill. Juv. has creamy yellow wash to underparts, contrasting with dark upperparts, and dark bill. Voice a repeated '*Vic-tor*'; also excited chattering call to guide people to beehives. **Status and habitat:** Common resident in woodland and savanna. Brood host of many cavity-nesting species. **SETSWANA: TSHÊTLHO**

### Bennett's Woodpecker
*Campethera bennettii*

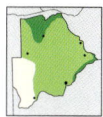

**22–24 cm** A medium-sized woodpecker with green-and-gold-barred upperparts, *spotted underparts,* and *plain face and throat.* Male has red crown and malar stripe; female has white-spotted dark forecrown, red hind crown, and brown cheek patch and throat. Like Golden-tailed Woodpecker, but underparts spotted (not streaked) with plain (not streaked) face. A plain (unspotted) subspecies occurs in the north. **Status and habitat:** Common resident in savanna and woodland. **SETSWANA: QOQONAMUTI**

### Golden-tailed Woodpecker
*Campethera abingoni*

**19–22 cm** A medium-sized woodpecker with green–gold -spotted upperparts, *heavily streaked underparts, forming gorget on throat,* and *lightly streaked cheeks.* Male has red crown with heavy dark streaks on forecrown, and red malar stripe; female has black-and-white-spotted forecrown and red hind crown, and streaked malar stripe. Similar to Bennett's Woodpecker. **Status and habitat:** Common resident in woodland and savanna. **SETSWANA: KOKOMORE**

## Bearded Woodpecker
*Chloropicus namaquus*

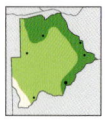

**23–25 cm** A *large woodpecker* with lightly barred grey-green and gold upperparts, heavily barred grey-and-white underparts, and *boldly marked face pattern* with black eye-stripe and malar stripe contrasting with white cheeks. Male has black-and-white-spotted forecrown, and red hind crown merging into black nape; female lacks red in crown. **Status and habitat:** Common resident in mature woodland and riparian forest. **SETSWANA: KOKOMORE**

## Cardinal Woodpecker
*Dendropicos fuscescens*

**14–16 cm** A small woodpecker with *lightly barred green back, dark-streaked pale underparts*, and black moustachial stripe. Male has bright red crown with brown forecrown; female has black crown with brown forecrown. **Status and habitat:** Common resident in wooded habitat, including savanna, forest edge and suburbia. **SETSWANA: KOKOMORE**

## Chinspot Batis
*Batis molitor*

**13 cm** A small black-and-white flycatcher-like bird with *broad black breast band*, grey crown and mantle, and *crisp white underparts*. Female has *broad chestnut breast band and obvious chestnut chin spot* (hence name). Male almost identical to male Pririt Batis, but has *plain* white (not dark-mottled) flanks; best separated by voice, which is a descending, whistled 'three-blind-mice'. **Status and habitat:** Common resident throughout savanna and woodland, particularly favouring acacia woodland. **SETSWANA: JÔKÔSEKÊI**

## Pririt Batis
*Batis pririt*

**12 cm** A small black-and-white flycatcher-like bird with *broad black breast band*, grey crown and mantle, and white underparts *with dark-mottled flanks*. Female lacks breast band and has plain buff-yellow underparts. Male best differentiated from Chinspot Batis by voice, which is a descending series of whistles. **Status and habitat:** Common resident in semi-arid woodland and riparian vegetation in arid areas. **SETSWANA: JÔKÔSEKÊI**

## Orange-breasted Bushshrike
*Chlorophoneus sulfureopectus*

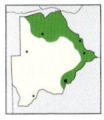

**19 cm** A bright, colourful bushshrike with *mostly green upperparts, yellow underparts with orange wash on breast*, grey nape and crown, yellow forehead and face, and dark eye-stripe. More likely to be heard than seen; voice a high-pitched and excited whistled 'woo-woo-woo-wooooo', with emphasis on the final note. **Status and habitat:** Common resident in woodland and savanna.
**SETSWANA: NAME UNKNOWN**

## Black-crowned Tchagra
*Tchagra senegalus*

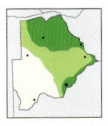

**21–22 cm** A medium-sized bushshrike with mostly dark brown upperparts, chestnut wings, *black crown, obvious dark eye-stripe,* and pale brown underparts. In flight, white-tipped tail is conspicuous. Similar to Brown-crowned Tchagra (p. 86) but with black (not brown) crown. Song is a high-pitched series of mournful warbling whistles.
**Status and habitat:** Common resident in the understorey of woodland and savanna.
**SETSWANA: PHÊNAKGÔMO**

### Brown-crowned Tchagra
*Tchagra australis*

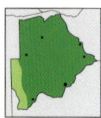

**18 cm** A medium-sized, mostly brown bushshrike with mostly dark brown upperparts, chestnut wings, *dark-bordered brown crown*, *obvious dark eye-stripe,* and pale brown underparts. In flight, white-tipped tail is conspicuous. Very similar to Black-crowned Tchagra (p. 85). Song mostly given from a display flight, which includes wing claps and a repeated, descending musical 'chee-wee'. **Status and habitat:** Common resident in the understorey of woodland and savanna. SETSWANA: **PHÊNAKGÔMO**

### Black-backed Puffback
*Dryoscopus cubla*

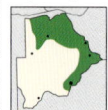

**17 cm** A small *black-and-white bushshrike* with an *obvious red eye*. Displaying male puffs out white lower back feathers, producing a white 'puffball'. Female and juv. duller, with light buffy underparts and pale supercilium. Superficially similar to Brubru, but lacks chestnut flanks. Voice highly variable, but mostly includes various clicks and a whistled 'chu-weee'. **Status and habitat:** Common resident in woodland and riparian forest. SETSWANA: **TLÊNTLÊRÊHUU**

### Swamp Boubou  *Laniarius bicolor*

**23–25 cm** A striking bushshrike with *pure white underparts, and black upperparts* with white wing bar. Voice a duet, with male uttering a deep, mournful whistle and female responding with a loud rattle. Superficially similar to Southern Fiscal (p. 89), but separated by shorter tail, horizontal stance and habit of feeding in the undergrowth. **Status and habitat:** Common resident in thick vegetation near rivers and swamps. SETSWANA: **SASOO**

## Crimson-breasted Shrike
*Laniarius atrococcineus*

**22–25 cm** A striking bushshrike with *bright red underparts and black upperparts* with white wing bar. Rare yellow morph with bright yellow underparts. Regularly forages in undergrowth and on the ground. Voice a loud series of pops, whistles and rattles. **Status and habitat:** Common and widespread resident in woodland, particularly favouring thorn trees.
SETSWANA: **KGARAGOBA**

## Brubru
*Nilaus afer*

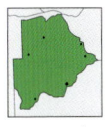

**14 cm** A small, mostly *black-and-white bushshrike with chestnut flanks, white wing bar and pale supercilium*. Female has browner upperparts, duller underparts, with light streaking to breast and face. Superficially similar to Black-backed Puffback. Voice a trilled 'prrrrrr'. **Status and habitat:** Common resident in woodland and savanna. SETSWANA: **NAME UNKNOWN**

## White-crested Helmetshrike
*Prionops plumatus*

**18 cm** An unusual-looking helmetshrike with mostly black upperparts with obvious white wing bar, grey crown, *black ear coverts, yellow eyes and eye wattle,* and white underparts. In flight, white wing bar and white-bordered black tail are obvious. Voice a series of croaks, buzzes and clicks. A highly gregarious species found in small noisy flocks. **Status and habitat:** Common resident, mostly in broadleaved woodland and savanna. SETSWANA: **LE.RANTHATA**

### Retz's Helmetshrike  *Prionops retzii*

**20–22 cm** A mostly black helmetshrike with *yellow eyes, red eye wattle and bill,* and white vent. In flight, white wing bar and white-bordered black tail obvious. Voice various rasps and buzzes. A highly gregarious species found in small noisy flocks. **Status and habitat:** Uncommon resident in tall, broadleaved woodland and riparian forest.
**SETSWANA: NAME UNKNOWN**

### Black Cuckooshrike *Campephaga flava*

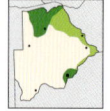

**18–21 cm** An *all-dark cuckooshrike with slight metallic gloss to plumage, and a yellow gape.* Male may show bright yellow shoulder patch. Female mostly brown, heavily barred below with yellow-edged wing feathers; dull yellow underwings evident only in flight. Superficially similar to Southern Black Flycatcher (p. 116); easily separated from Fork-tailed Drongo (p. 91) by square-ended tail. Voice a very high-pitched trill. **Status and habitat:** Common resident and summer migrant in woodland, savanna and riparian forest. **SETSWANA: NAME UNKNOWN**

### Southern White-crowned Shrike
*Eurocephalus anguitimens*

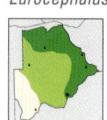

**23–25 cm** A large, heavyset shrike with brown upperparts, white underparts, *large dark ear coverts and white crown.* Mostly found in small noisy groups. Voice a harsh, loud '*kee-kee-kee*'. **Status and habitat:** Common resident in woodland and savanna, both acacia and broadleaved.
**SETSWANA: LE.NKUTSHWÊU**

## Magpie Shrike  *Lanius melanoleucus*

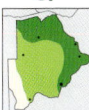

**40–50 cm (incl. tail)** An easily recognisable, *long-tailed black shrike* with white lower back and wing bar. Occurs in small groups, calling loudly and perching prominently. Voice includes various loud, liquid whistles. **Status and habitat:** Common resident in acacia savanna, occasionally found in broadleaved woodland. **SETSWANA: TILODI**

## Southern Fiscal  *Lanius collaris*

**21–23 cm** A medium-sized black-and-white shrike with *longish tail, white scapular bar and obvious white supercilium*. Female has small chestnut patch on lower flanks. Juv. has grey-brown upperparts, and light barring and scaling above and below. Ad. most similar to Fiscal Flycatcher (p. 116); superficially similar to Swamp Boubou (p. 86); juv. similar to Lesser Grey and Red-backed shrikes (p. 90). **Status and habitat:** Uncommon resident in a variety of open woodland habitats. **SETSWANA: TLHÔMÊDI**

## Lesser Grey Shrike  *Lanius minor*

**20–22 cm** A medium-sized shrike with *grey mantle, nape, hind crown and rump*, black wings, tail and mask, and white underparts. Juv. has reduced black on forecrown; similar to juv. Southern Fiscal, but upperparts only very lightly barred and lacks brown tones. **Status and habitat:** Common Palearctic-br. summer migrant occurring in open and semi-arid savanna. **SETSWANA: NAME UNKNOWN**

### Red-backed Shrike  *Lanius collurio*

**18 cm** A strikingly patterned shrike with *chestnut back and wings, grey crown, nape and rump*, and black mask. Female considerably duller, with scaled underparts, grey-brown crown, and mask restricted to ear coverts. Female similar to juv. Southern Fiscal (p. 89(, but with chestnut upperparts (lacking pale wing bar) and shorter tail. **Status and habitat:** Common Palearctic-br. summer migrant occurring in open and semi-arid savanna. SETSWANA: NAME UNKNOWN

### African Golden Oriole  *Oriolus auratus*

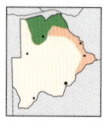

**20–24 cm** A *mostly golden-yellow* oriole with *yellow head, black eye-stripe* and bright red bill. Female less brightly coloured, with greenish tinge to upperparts, and lightly streaked underparts. Similar to Eurasian Golden Oriole but with more yellow (not black) wings. Voice a series of liquid whistles, as well as harsh squawks. **Status and habitat:** Common to uncommon resident and intra-African br. migrant found in tall broadleaved woodland and riparian forest. SETSWANA: NAME UNKNOWN

### Eurasian Golden Oriole  *Oriolus oriolus*

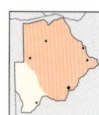

**22–25 cm** A golden-yellow oriole with *mostly black wings, black lores* and bright red bill. Female much duller, with green-yellow upperparts, and *pale underparts with fine dark streaks*. Similar to African Golden Oriole, but with black restricted to front of eye; male has more black in wings; female has paler yellow underparts with heavier streaking. Voice a series of liquid whistles, as well as harsh squawks. **Status and habitat:** Common Palearctic-br. summer migrant in woodland and savanna. SETSWANA: NAME UNKNOWN

## Black-headed Oriole  *Oriolus larvatus*

**20–24 cm** An unmistakable, brightly coloured *golden-yellow oriole with black head*, green-yellow upperparts, and red bill. In flight, dark flight feathers and green-yellow tail obvious. Voice a series of liquid whistles, as well as harsh squawks. **Status and habitat:** Common resident in moist woodland, riparian forest and suburbia. SETSWANA: **NAME UNKNOWN**

## Fork-tailed Drongo  *Dicrurus adsimilis*

**23–26 cm** A medium-sized, *all-black bird with longish, deeply forked tail*. In flight, shows paler flight feathers. Most similar to Southern Black Flycatcher (p. 116); also similar to dark-plumaged Black Cuckooshrike (p. 88), but easily separated by deeply forked tail. Voice includes a range of creaks and other harsh notes; regularly mimics other bird species. **Status and habitat:** Very common and widespread resident in savanna, woodland and suburbia. SETSWANA: **SE.ROTHÊ**

## Cape Crow  *Corvus capensis*

**45–50 cm** The *only all-black crow in Botswana*. Has glossy plumage and long, slender bill. Unlikely to be mistaken for any other species. Voice includes harsh cawing and unusual liquid sounds. **Status and habitat:** Common resident in most open habitats, including grassland, agricultural land and desert; often seen perching and nesting on roadside poles and pylons. SETSWANA: **LE.GAKABÊ**

## Pied Crow
*Corvus albus*

**46–50 cm** An unmistakable *black-and-white crow with obvious white breast and collar*. Voice includes an assortment of harsh caws. **Status and habitat:** Very common resident across most habitats, except deserts. Well adapted to human settlements, where it may occur in high densities. **SETSWANA: LE.GAKABÊ**

## Southern Black Tit
*Melaniparus niger*

**16 cm** A *black tit with obvious white shoulder, wing panel* and outer tail feathers and white-barred vent. Female has slightly paler underparts. Voice an excited assortment of harsh 'chee-chee-chee' notes and whistled musical vocalisations. **Status and habitat:** Common resident in moist broadleaved woodland and savanna. **SETSWANA: NAME UNKNOWN**

## Ashy Tit
*Melaniparus cinerascens*

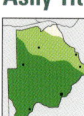

**15 cm** A grey tit with *mostly black head, obvious white cheek patch*, and broad black stripe down the chest. Unlikely to be mistaken for any other tit species in Botswana. Voice a mix of harsh trills and whistles. **Status and habitat:** Common resident in acacia woodland and thornveld, particularly in the Kalahari. **SETSWANA: SE.BATALEDI**

## Cape Penduline Tit
*Anthoscopus minutus*

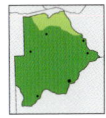

**8–10 cm** A tiny tit with grey-brown upperparts, *dull yellow underparts, black-and-white-scaled forehead and sharp, delicate bill.* Similar to Yellow-bellied Eremomela (p. 109). Constructs elaborate nest, made of woolly plant matter, with false entrance and sealable entrance tunnel. **Status and habitat:** Common resident in semi-arid shrubland and acacia savanna. SETSWANA: **SE.SETLO**

## Chestnut-backed Sparrow-Lark
*Eremopterix leucotis*

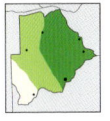

**12–13 cm** A strikingly patterned lark with *chestnut back, black underparts and head, and white ear and nape patches.* Female has grey-brown head, pale nuchal collar and heavily streaked and blotched underparts. Like Grey-backed Sparrow-Lark; male told apart by separate white ear and nape patches, and chestnut back; female by chestnut back and complete nuchal collar. **Status and habitat:** Common resident and nomad in semi-arid savanna and fallow agricultural land. SETSWANA: **TSHILWANE**

## Grey-backed Sparrow-Lark
*Eremopterix verticalis*

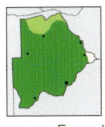

**12–13 cm** A pale-and-black lark with *pale grey back, black underparts, black face with white crown and white ear patch extending onto nape.* Female mostly brown with partial pale collar, dark-streaked underparts and black lower belly. Both sexes similar to Chestnut-backed Sparrow-Lark. **Status and habitat:** Common resident and nomad in arid and semi-arid plains and grassland, as well as fallow agricultural land. SETSWANA: **TSHILWANE**

## Dusky Lark  *Pinarocorys nigricans*

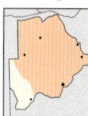

**19–20 cm** A large lark with *dark brown upperparts* with pale-tipped wing fringes, and pale underparts with *dark spots to throat, breast and face*. Superficially similar to larger Groundscraper Thrush (p. 114), but has darker upperparts and different facial markings. While foraging, continually raises wings. **Status and habitat:** Uncommon African-br. summer migrant occurring in open and heavily grassed savanna and woodland. **SETSWANA: SE.BOTA**

## Spike-heeled Lark
*Chersomanes albofasciata*

**13–15 cm** A small lark with *long, decurved bill,* dark brown scalloped upperparts, and *pale sandy brown underparts* with white throat and very lightly streaked upper chest. Very *short, white-tipped tail* most obvious in flight. Often seen in small groups, when excited trill call is given. Similar to other lark species, but easily distinguished by long, decurved bill and short, white-tipped tail. **Status and habitat:** Common resident in arid and semi-arid grassland and shrubland. **SETSWANA: SE.BOTA**

## Sabota Lark  *Calendulauda sabota*

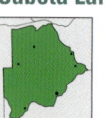

**15 cm** A medium-sized lark *with strong supercilium, boldly marked face (including moustachial stripe), pale underparts and dark streaking to upper chest*. Very similar to Fawn-coloured Lark; best separated by more boldly marked facial patterning, darker streaking to underparts and voice. Voice a series of jumbling notes; regularly includes mimicry. **Status and habitat:** Common resident across bushveld and arid savanna. **SETSWANA: SE.BOTA**

## Fawn-coloured Lark
*Calendulauda africanoides*

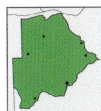

**14–16 cm** A medium-sized lark with *bold supercilium, plain face* (generally lacking moustachial stripe), rufous wing panel, and pale underparts with *thin streaks to upper chest*. Very similar to Sabota Lark. Voice a musical twittering which ends in a buzzy note. **Status and habitat:** Common resident in Kalahari savanna and woodland, particularly in sandy soils. **SETSWANA: SE.BOTA**

## Eastern Clapper Lark  *Corypha fasciolata*

**14–15 cm** A mostly plain rufous lark with *heavy bill*, brown upperparts with *heavily patterned mantle and wing coverts*, and pale underparts with thinly dark-streaked chest. Similar to other lark species, most like Rufous-naped Lark (p. 96), but lacks crest and has shorter bill; best separated by *distinctive display*, clapping wings while ascending, then whistling while parachuting down. **Status and habitat:** Common resident in savanna, shrubland and grassland. **SETSWANA: NÔNYANE YAPULA**

## Monotonous Lark  *Mirafra passerina*

**14 cm** A fairly nondescript plump lark with *heavy conical bill*, dark upperparts, pale underparts with lightly dark-streaked chest, and *contrastingly white throat,* which is puffed out while giving display song (when *short crest* may be seen). Similar to other lark species and most easily recognised when giving short display flight or when singing from bushes. Song is a series of repeated croaky notes rendered 'for-syrup-is-sweet'. **Status and habitat:** Uncommon nomad in open savanna; may occur in large numbers in wet years. **SETSWANA: SE.BOTA**

### Rufous-naped Lark — *Corypha africana*

**15–18 cm** A large lark with *erectile head crest, longish heavy bill, rufous wing patches*, and light brown underparts with dark streaks on chest. Similar to Eastern Clapper (p. 95) and Short-clawed larks. Voice a musical high-pitched, three-toned whistle, mostly sung from a prominent perch. **Status and habitat:** Common resident in grassland and open savanna. SETSWANA: SE.BOTÊKGÔMO

### Short-clawed Lark — *Certhilauda chuana*

**17–19 cm** A large, slim lark with *longish, slender bill, buffy supercilium*, heavily scaled and streaked mantle and finely streaked upper chest. Similar to heavier-set Rufous-naped Lark, but lacks rufous wing panel in folded wing and erectile crest. Voice a long, wispy whistle given whilst perched or in stooping aerial display. **Status and habitat:** Highly localised but common resident in the southeast, favouring open savanna with low bushes. SETSWANA: SE.BOTA

### Red-capped Lark — *Calandrella cinerea*

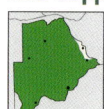

**14–16 cm** A medium-sized pale lark with obvious *rufous cap and shoulder patch*, and *whitish underparts without any streaking*, which helps distinguish it from other lark species. Often found in small, highly mobile flocks. Voice a sparrow-like chirp, with various high-pitched notes, given in display flight. **Status and habitat:** Common resident and nomad in grassland, semi-arid savanna and fallow agricultural land. SETSWANA: SE.BOTA

## African Pipit  *Anthus cinnamomeus*

**16–17 cm** A common pipit with pale supercilium and bold facial patterning, *yellowish base to bill, well-marked mantle, heavily streaked chest and white outer tail feathers*. Separated from lark species by more erect stance, longer legs and more slender shape; similar to Buffy Pipit. **Status and habitat:** Common resident in most open habitats with short grass, including grassland, open patches in savanna, agricultural land and even playing fields. SETSWANA: KELEMA-KELE-NÔSI

## Buffy Pipit  *Anthus vaalensis*

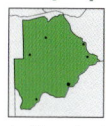

**18–19 cm** A rather large, heavyset pipit with pale supercilium and relatively plain face, *pinkish base to bill, mostly plain mantle, and buffy outer tail feathers*. Separated from lark species by more erect stance, and longer legs; similar to African Pipit, but separated by pinkish bill base, mostly plain mantle and buffy outer tail feathers. **Status and habitat:** Common to uncommon resident and nomad of open habitats, including grassy plains, fallow agricultural land, and overgrazed and recently burnt land. SETSWANA: NAME UNKNOWN

## Cape Wagtail  *Motacilla capensis*

**20 cm** A mostly *grey-brown wagtail* with white underparts and dark, V-shaped breast band (southern/eastern subspecies) or breast spot (northern subspecies). Like other wagtail species, it constantly wags its long, pale-edged tail, hence the name. May be mistaken for greyer-toned juv. African Pied Wagtail (p. 98), but lacks obvious white wing panel. **Status and habitat:** Common resident in aquatic habitats, as well as human-modified habitats, including lawns and parks. SETSWANA: MO.SALAKATANE

WAGTAIL, BULBULS

### African Pied Wagtail *Motacilla aguimp*

**20 cm** A striking *black-and-white wagtail with white wing panel*, boldly marked face, and black breast band. Juv. like ad. but with grey-black upperparts; confusion possible with Cape Wagtail (p. 97). Like other wagtail species, it continuously wags its long, white-edged tail, hence the name. **Status and habitat:** Common resident in aquatic habitats, such as shorelines of large water bodies and river banks, and human-modified habitats, such as lawns and parks. **SETSWANA: MO.SALAKATANE**

### African Red-eyed Bulbul
*Pycnonotus nigricans*

**20 cm** A distinctive-looking bulbul with *black head and crest, red eyes with bright orange-red eye-ring, contrastingly pale underparts* and yellow vent. Superficially similar to Dark-capped Bulbul, but easily separated by red eyes and eye-ring and paler underparts. **Status and habitat:** Very common and widespread resident of arid and semi-arid savanna and woodland, and suburban gardens. **SETSWANA: MARITINKÔLE**

### Dark-capped Bulbul
*Pycnonotus tricolor*

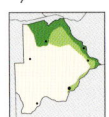

**20–21 cm** A common bulbul with *black head and crest, dark eyes and eye-ring*, and yellow vent. Similar to African Red-eyed Bulbul. **Status and habitat:** Common resident in slightly lusher wooded habitats than African Red-eyed Bulbul, including savanna and suburban gardens. **SETSWANA: MARITINKÔLE**

## Terrestrial Brownbul
*Phyllastrephus terrestris*

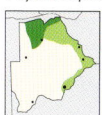

**18–22 cm** A medium-sized bulbul with *plain brown upperparts, light brown underparts and contrasting white throat*. A highly vocal species that occurs in noisy groups, uttering various harsh '*brrrr*' notes. **Status and habitat:** Common resident in the undergrowth of dense woodland, thickets and riparian forest. **SETSWANA: MARITINKOLÊ**

## Yellow-bellied Greenbul
*Chlorocichla flaviventris*

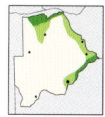

**20–23 cm** A medium-sized bulbul with plain brown upperparts, *plain yellow underparts*, longish, heavy bill, and *whitish eye-ring*, most prominent above the eye. Song a repeated nasal '*ha-ha-ha*' and loud churring. **Status and habitat:** Common resident in moist woodland and riparian forest. **SETSWANA: NAME UNKNOWN**

## Banded Martin
*Neophedina cincta*

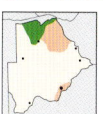

**15–17 cm** A large, heavyset martin with brown upperparts, *small white supercilium*, and white underparts with *broad breast band and vent band*. In flight, shows *pale underwing coverts*, and square-ended tail. Similar to smaller Sand Martin (p. 100), which lacks pale supercilium and vent band, and has forked tail and dark underwing coverts. **Status and habitat:** Common resident and intra-African br. summer migrant occurring in grassland, shrubland and floodplains. **SETSWANA: PÊOLANE**

### Sand Martin *Riparia riparia*

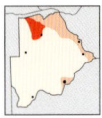

**12–13 cm** A small martin with brown upperparts, and white underparts with *dark breast band*; often shows faint pale nuchal collar. In flight, shows *entirely dark underwings*. Similar to Banded Martin (p. 99), and Brown-throated Martin, which has an entirely dark throat. **Status and habitat:** Uncommon Palearctic-br. summer migrant found in water-associated habitats, including marshes, wetlands, floodplains and sewage works. **SETSWANA: PÊOLANE**

dark morph

white-bellied morph

### Brown-throated Martin
*Riparia paludicola*

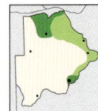

**12 cm** A very small, delicate martin occurring in two colour morphs: an *all-dark brown morph* and a *white-bellied morph*, which has white belly and vent. Superficially similar to Sand Martin. **Status and habitat:** Common resident associated with aquatic habitats, including wetlands, dams, rivers and sewage works, although regularly seen foraging well away from water. **SETSWANA: PÊOLANE**

### Western House Martin
*Delichon urbicum*

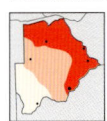

**14 cm** A striking martin with *glossy blue-black upperparts* (may lose gloss, becoming brown-grey) *with obvious white rump* and pearly white underparts. If perched, the white-feathered legs and toes may be obvious. Similar to Pearl-breasted Swallow, but easily separated by obvious white rump. **Status and habitat:** Uncommon Palearctic-br. summer migrant found in a variety of open habitats, including savanna, open woodland, floodplains, agricultural land and grassland. **SETSWANA: PÊOLANE**

## Pearl-breasted Swallow
*Hirundo dimidiata*

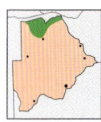

**13–14 cm** A small, dainty swallow with *uniform glossy blue upperparts, pure white underparts* (lacking any bands), and shallowly forked tail. Similar to Western House Martin; separated from Wire-tailed Swallow by lack of rufous cap, long tail streamers and dark vent band. **Status and habitat:** Uncommon resident and intra-African non-br. summer migrant found in shrubland, savanna and agricultural land; regularly occurs near open water bodies. **SETSWANA: PÊOLANE**

## Wire-tailed Swallow *Hirundo smithii*

**16–18 cm (incl. tail streamers)** A small, delicate swallow with *rufous cap*, metallic blue upperparts, white underparts, *dark vent band and long, thin tail streamers* (which may be tricky to see in flight). Similar to Pearl-breasted Swallow and superficially similar to Barn Swallow, but easily separated by rufous cap and mostly white underparts. Juv. similar to ad. but with grey-brown cap and reduced tail streamers. **Status and habitat:** Common resident near to water bodies, including rivers, streams and dams. **SETSWANA: PÊOLANE**

## Barn Swallow *Hirundo rustica*

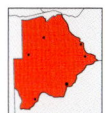

**15–20 cm (incl. tail streamers)** A medium-sized swallow with metallic blue upperparts, *rufous throat, broad, dark breast band*, off-white belly and long tail streamers. Juv. similar to ad. but with pale forehead, buff-white throat and duller upperparts. Superficially similar to Wire-tailed Swallow. **Status and habitat:** Very common and widespread Palearctic-br. summer migrant, which may be seen in all habitats but scarce in desert. **SETSWANA: PÊOLANE**

ad.

juv.

### Lesser Striped Swallow
*Cecropis abyssinica*

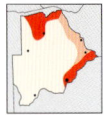

**15–19 cm (incl. tail streamers)**
A medium-sized swallow with *boldly streaked underparts, dark rufous cap, cheeks, and rump*, metallic blue back and wings, and very long tail streamers. May be confused with Greater Striped Swallow, but has rufous cheeks and bolder-streaked underparts. Juv. like ad. but with shorter tail streamers. **Status and habitat:** Common br. intra-African summer visitor found in most open habitats, including grassland, savanna and rural settlements; often near to water. **SETSWANA: PÊOLANE**

### Greater Striped Swallow
*Cecropis cucullata*

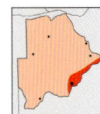

**16–20 cm (incl. tail streamers)**
A large swallow with *thinly streaked underparts, light orange-rufous cap and rump, pale cheeks* and metallic blue back. Similar to smaller Lesser Striped Swallow. Juv. like ad. but with shorter tail streamers. **Status and habitat:** Common intra-African summer visitor, breeding only in the southeast. Found in most open habitats, including grassland, savanna, agricultural land and suburbia. **SETSWANA: PÊOLANE**

### Red-breasted Swallow
*Cecropis semirufa*

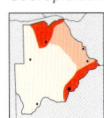

**22–24 cm** A large, highly distinctive swallow with dark blue upperparts and ear coverts, *rich rufous underparts* and rump, and *long, thin tail streamers*. Separated from other swallow species by entirely rufous underparts. **Status and habitat:** Common intra-African br. summer migrant in open savanna and grassland. **SETSWANA: PÊOLANE**

## Long-billed Crombec
*Sylvietta rufescens*

**11 cm** A small, plump, *very short-tailed bird* with grey upperparts, buffy-rufous underparts, dark eye-stripe and *long bill*. Almost tailless appearance differentiates it from other small warbler-like birds, although superficially similar to Burnt-necked Eremomela (p. 109). Voice a loud repeated 'chip-chirrit-chirrit'. **Status and habitat:** Common resident in shrubland, savanna and woodland. **SETSWANA: POPONAKA**

## Little Rush Warbler
*Bradypterus baboecala*

**14–17 cm** A large warbler with *dark brown upperparts*, *finely streaked breast*, buffy vent, and *longish, heavy tail*. Voice an accelerating 'chip chip chip-chip-chip-chi-ch-chii' ending in a trill. Similar to Lesser Swamp Warbler, but darker, with finely streaked breast and different voice. **Status and habitat:** Common resident in reed beds, papyrus swamps and other thick aquatic vegetation. **SETSWANA: KGWARAKGWÊTLHANE**

## Lesser Swamp Warbler
*Acrocephalus gracilirostris*

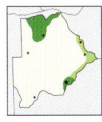

**14–17 cm** A large warbler with *warm brown upperparts*, *strong white supercilium*, *plain whitish underparts*, and *longish bill*. Most similar to smaller Common Reed Warbler (p. 104), but with whiter underparts, longer bill and different voice; also similar to Little Rush Warbler. Voice a series of loud, melodic liquid notes and trills. **Status and habitat:** Common resident in aquatic habitats, including reed beds, swamps and other aquatic vegetation. **SETSWANA: KGWARAKGWÊTLHANE**

## Common Reed Warbler
*Acrocephalus scirpaceus*

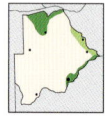

**12–13 cm** A small warbler with *light brown upperparts*, pale supercilium, *buffy flanks, whitish throat*, and pale chest and belly. Confusion likely with other reed-dwelling warblers, but separated by smaller size, lighter brown upperparts and buffy flanks. **Status and habitat:** Common resident and intra-African br. migrant. Mostly found near water such as in reed beds and water-associated scrub and tall grass. SETSWANA: **KGWARAKGWÊTLHANE**

## Willow Warbler  *Phylloscopus trochilus*

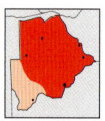

**12 cm** A small warbler with a *strong, pale yellow supercilium* (extending well past eye), *dark eye-stripe*, grey upperparts and lighter underparts, often with *dull yellow wash*. Similar to slightly larger Icterine Warbler but lacks pale eye-ring and has strong supercilium and eye-stripe. Voice a strong musical descending song with a commonly heard '*wooo-eeet*' contact note. **Status and habitat:** Common Palearctic-br. summer migrant found in a variety of wooded habitats. SETSWANA: **KGWARAKGWÊTLHANE**

## Icterine Warbler  *Hippolais icterina*

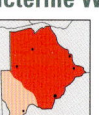

**13–14 cm** A smallish warbler with light brown upperparts with pale wing panel, *dull yellow underparts*, *plain face with pale lores and eye-ring*, and pinkish bill. Similar to smaller Willow Warbler. Voice a warbling, jumble of melodious notes with many harsh '*weeee*' notes. **Status and habitat:** Common Palearctic-br. summer migrant occurring in a variety of wooded habitats, such as woodland, savanna and riparian vegetation. SETSWANA: **KGWARAKGWÊTLHANE**

CISTICOLAS 105

### Rattling Cisticola — *Cisticola chiniana*

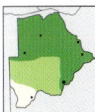

**15 cm** A medium-sized cisticola with *rufous-brown crown*, *palish bill*, boldly marked mantle, and rufous wing panel. Very similar to Tinkling Cisticola, but lacks strong supercilium and has paler bill; also similar to Chirping Cisticola. *Voice distinctive:* a harsh '*churr-churr-churr*' followed by a short rattle; voice is the most reliable method to distinguish cisticolas. **Status and habitat:** Common resident in savanna and open woodland. SETSWANA: TÔNTÔSI

### Tinkling Cisticola — *Cisticola rufilatus*

**14 cm** A medium-sized cisticola with *rufous crown*, *obvious pale supercilium*, boldly marked mantle and *thinnish dark bill*. Similar to Tawny-flanked Prinia (p. 107), but has marked mantle, shorter tail, rufous cap and noticeably different voice; also similar to Rattling and Chirping cisticolas. Voice a strong trill and high-pitched '*twee-twee-twee*' notes. **Status and habitat:** Common to uncommon resident in broadleaved woodland and savanna. SETSWANA: TÔNTÔSI

### Chirping Cisticola — *Cisticola pipiens*

**14 cm** A medium-sized cisticola with obvious *rusty cap* and indistinct supercilium, *broad black streaking on mantle*, and longish tail with paler tip. Similar to Rattling and Tinkling cisticolas, but separated by dark-patterned mantle, habitat and voice. Voice a '*chip-chip-chip-churrrrrrrr*' with emphasis on the final trill. **Status and habitat:** Common resident in reed beds and other aquatic vegetation, favouring papyrus-dominated areas. SETSWANA: TÔNTÔSI

### Neddicky — *Cisticola fulvicapilla*

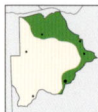

**11 cm** A small plain cisticola with *unmarked mantle, rufous cap*, short tail, and light grey-brown underparts. Separated from other smaller cisticola species by entirely unmarked mantle. Voice a repeated liquid '*tseep-tseep-tseep*' and a '*tic*' alarm note. **Status and habitat:** Common resident in savanna and woodland. **SETSWANA: TÔNTÔSI**

### Zitting Cisticola — *Cisticola juncidis*

**11 cm** A small light brown cisticola with *dark-streaked crown*, heavily streaked and patterned mantle, and *short tail, with white tip and dark subterminal band*. Almost identical to Desert Cisticola, but has marginally longer tail with more obvious black subterminal band; best separated by display song, which is given during an undulating display flight, uttering '*zit*' on each dip. **Status and habitat:** Common resident in tall grassland and agricultural land. **SETSWANA: TÔNTÔSI**

### Desert Cisticola — *Cisticola aridulus*

**11 cm** A small light brown cisticola with *dark-streaked crown*, patterned mantle and *shortish, white-tipped tail*. Almost identical to Zitting Cisticola and best differentiated by display song. Voice a high-pitched and fast '*wee-wee-wee*' given in display flight, as well as frantic clicks. **Status and habitat:** Common resident in dry grassland, grassy patches within savanna, and fallow agricultural land. **SETSWANA: TÔNTÔSI**

## Tawny-flanked Prinia  *Prinia subflava*

**13 cm** A slim bird with *long tail (usually held cocked), dark eye-stripe, pale supercilium*, plain brown back, russet wings, and pale underparts with light brown flanks. May be confused with non-br. and juv. Black-chested Prinia, but separated by russet wings and lack of yellow wash to underparts. Superficially similar to Tinkling Cisticola (p. 105). **Status and habitat:** Common resident in rank grass, scrub and bushes in woodland; normally close to water. **SETSWANA: TÔNTÔBANE**

## Black-chested Prinia  *Prinia flavicans*

**14 cm** A slim bird with *long tail (usually held cocked), white throat, and pale yellow underparts with broad black breast band*. Non-br. ad. and juv. lack breast band and have light yellow wash to underparts; similar to Tawny-flanked Prinia. **Status and habitat:** Common resident in arid wooded areas and savanna. **SETSWANA: TÔNTÔBANE**

## Rufous-eared Warbler
*Malcorus pectoralis*

**15 cm** A distinctive-looking, slim, long-tailed bird with *black breast band, rufous ear coverts*, white throat and greyish underparts. Juv. lacks breast band and has duller brown ear coverts. **Status and habitat:** Common resident in arid shrubland and semi-desert. **SETSWANA: NAME UNKNOWN**

### Yellow-breasted Apalis  *Apalis flavida*

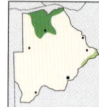

**12–13 cm** A small warbler-like bird with *green back and tail, grey head and face, red eyes,* and *yellow breast patch* with black breast spot or incomplete breast band. Female lacks black breast spot or breast band. Voice an excited, raspy, duetted '*chirrip-chirrip-chirrip*'. **Status and habitat:** Common resident in woodland and savanna.
**SETSWANA: NAME UNKNOWN**

### Grey-backed Camaroptera
*Camaroptera brevicaudata*

**12–13 cm** A small warbler-like bird with *grey tail (held cocked), grey back and head, green wings* and whitish underparts. More frequently heard than seen, when it gives a penetrating knocking '*prrrp-prrrp-prrrp*' song and nasal, bleating alarm call. **Status and habitat:** Common resident in woodland and thickets. **SETSWANA: NAME UNKNOWN**

### Barred Wren-Warbler
*Calamonastes fasciolatus*

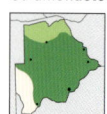

**14 cm** A small brown warbler with *dark-scaled throat* and *buffy underparts with heavy barring*. Non-br. male and female have paler underparts with less barring. Voice a liquid and musical repeated '*prrrup-prrrup-prrrup*'. **Status and habitat:** Common resident in arid woodland and savanna. **SETSWANA: NAME UNKNOWN**

## Yellow-bellied Eremomela
*Eremomela icteropygialis*

**10–11 cm** A small mostly grey warbler-like bird with obvious *yellow vent and belly*. Similar to Cape Penduline Tit (p. 93), but with yellow restricted to lower belly and vent and no scaling on forehead. Voice a cheerful, high-pitched song. **Status and habitat:** Common resident in arid and semi-arid shrubland and savanna. **SETSWANA: NAME UNKNOWN**

## Burnt-necked Eremomela
*Eremomela usticollis*

**10–11 cm** A small warbler-like bird with grey upperparts, *buffy underparts, often indistinct chestnut-brown cheek and breast patches, pale eyes* and pink bill. Coloration is similar to Long-billed Crombec (p. 103), but lacks obvious pale supercilium, and has longer tail, and brown cheek and breast patches. Voice a high-pitched, excited trill. **Status and habitat:** Common resident in savanna, particularly favouring acacia woodland. **SETSWANA: NAME UNKNOWN**

## Chestnut-vented Warbler
*Curruca subcoerulea*

**14–15 cm** A medium-sized, mostly grey warbler with *obvious chestnut vent, pale eyes, dark-streaked pale throat*, and dark grey tail with white tips and edges. Voice a powerful warbling song with many high pitched notes and trills. **Status and habitat:** Common resident in arid shrubland and acacia savanna. **SETSWANA: PARA-LANKU**

### Southern Yellow White-eye
*Zosterops anderssoni*

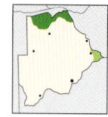

**11–12 cm** A *mostly bright yellow warbler-like bird* with slightly duller yellow-green upperparts, and *complete, obvious white eye-ring*, with slightly darker lores. Voice a cheerful warbling song. **Status and habitat:** Common resident in woodland, riparian forest and suburban gardens. SETSWANA: NAME UNKNOWN

### Arrow-marked Babbler
*Turdoides jardineii*

**22–25 cm** A mostly brown babbler with obvious *white arrow-shaped marks to head and underparts*, and red eyes with yellow inner ring. Similar to Hartlaub's Babbler but has clear arrow markings (not light scaling) on underparts, and dark (not white) rump and vent. Found in noisy groups. Voice a loud, harsh babbling. **Status and habitat:** Common resident in savanna and riparian woodland, particularly favouring areas with thickets. SETSWANA: LE.TSHÊGANÔGA

### Southern Pied Babbler
*Turdoides bicolor*

**23–26 cm** A black-and-white babbler with *all-white body and black wings and tail*. Occurs in noisy groups. Juv. plain brown, with slightly darker brown upperparts. Voice a raucous babbling. **Status and habitat:** Common resident in arid savanna, particularly favouring acacia savanna. SETSWANA: LE.TSHÊGANÔGA

BABBLER, MYNA, STARLING

## Hartlaub's Babbler  *Turdoides hartlaubii*

**24–26 cm** A brown babbler with *white-scaled underparts, head and mantle, white rump and vent*, and deep red eyes. Found in noisy groups. Voice a loud babbling. Similar to Arrow-marked Babbler. **Status and habitat:** Common resident in woodland and riparian forest close to water. SETSWANA: LE.TSHÊGANÔGA

## Common Myna  *Acridotheres tristis*

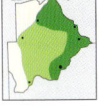

**23–25 cm** A striking, medium-sized starling-like bird with *dark brown body, blackish head and neck, and bare yellow ear coverts, bill and legs*. In flight, shows obvious white wing patches and tail tip. **Status and habitat:** Common introduced resident strongly associated with human modified environments, including suburbia and cities. SETSWANA: NAME UNKNOWN

## Wattled Starling  *Creatophora cinerea*

**21 cm** An unusual-looking pale starling with *bare black-and-yellow face with long black wattles*, mostly grey body, black wings and *white rump*. Non-br. male, female and juv. darker grey-brown, with feathered head and small bare yellow patch behind eye. **Status and habitat:** Common resident and nomad occurring in savanna and dry woodland. SETSWANA: PÔNYANE

### Cape Starling     *Lamprotornis nitens*

**23–25 cm** A medium-sized, short-tailed, metallic blue-green starling with *uniform head, indistinctly marked wings and bright orange eyes*. Very similar to Greater Blue-eared Starling, but has plain (not dark) ear coverts, indistinct (not obvious) spots on wing coverts, and green (not blue) flanks. **Status and habitat:** Common resident in savanna, woodland and suburbia.
SETSWANA: LE.GÔDI

### Greater Blue-eared Starling
*Lamprotornis chalybaeus*

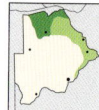

**22–24 cm** A medium-sized, short-tailed metallic blue-green starling with *dark ear coverts*, one or two *distinct rows of dark spots in wing coverts,* and blue flanks. May be confused with Cape Starling. **Status and habitat:** Common resident in savanna, woodland and even riparian forest. SETSWANA: LE.GÔDI

### Meves's Starling     *Lamprotornis mevesii*

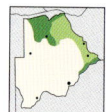

**34 cm** A medium-sized, *long-tailed* metallic purple-blue starling with dark eyes and ear coverts. May be confused with Burchell's Starling, which is bulkier, with shorter, more rounded tail and broader wings. **Status and habitat:** Common resident in mature woodland and riparian forest.
SETSWANA: NAME UNKNOWN

## Burchell's Starling
*Lamprotornis australis*

**32 cm** A large, *heavyset* blue-green starling with *longish, slightly rounded tail*, dark eyes and ear coverts, and *upright stance*. In flight, shows noticeably broad wings. May be confused with Meves's Starling. **Status and habitat:** Common resident in savanna and woodland. **SETSWANA: LE.GÔDI**

## Violet-backed Starling
*Cinnyricinclus leucogaster*

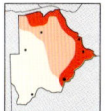

**17–18 cm** A small, striking starling with *violet upperparts, head and chest and otherwise white underparts*. Female has light brown back with dark-streaked white underparts. Female may be confused with Groundscraper Thrush (p. 114), which has heavier spots and streaks to underparts, and dark smudges below eyes. **Status and habitat:** Common intra-African br. summer migrant in woodland and riparian forest. **SETSWANA: REOLE**

## Red-winged Starling
*Onychognathus morio*

**28–30 cm** A medium-sized, *glossy black* starling with dark eyes, *obvious chestnut primaries* (most evident in flight) and longish, graduated tail. Female has light grey head. **Status and habitat:** Common localised resident in mountainous and rocky areas, as well as urban and suburban areas, where it uses buildings for nesting. **SETSWANA: LETSÔPI**

## Yellow-billed Oxpecker
*Buphagus africanus*

**20 cm** A starling-like bird with red-and-yellow bill, *orange-red eyes (lacking an eye-ring) and pale rump*. May be confused with Red-billed Oxpecker, which has all-red bill, orange-red eyes with obvious yellow eye-ring, and dark rump. Strongly associated with large herbivores, which it grooms for ectoparasites. **Status and habitat:** Common to uncommon resident in savanna and open woodland. SETSWANA: KALA

## Red-billed Oxpecker
*Buphagus erythrorynchus*

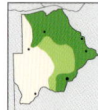

**19–20 cm** A starling-like bird with *all-red bill, orange eyes with broad yellow eye-ring, and dark rump*. Similar to Yellow-billed Oxpecker. Strongly associated with large herbivores, which it grooms for ectoparasites. **Status and habitat:** Common resident in savanna and woodland. SETSWANA: KALA

## Groundscraper Thrush
*Turdus litsitsirupa*

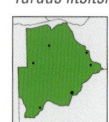

**21–23 cm** A *pale grey-brown* thrush with *black-spotted white underparts*, black smudges beneath the eye, and bi-coloured bill (orange below, dark above). In flight, pale orange wing patches obvious. Superficially similar to Dusky Lark (p. 94) and female Violet-backed Starling (p. 113). Often flicks wings (one or both) while foraging on the ground. **Status and habitat:** Common to uncommon resident in open woodland and even suburbia. SETSWANA: LE.TSUTSURÔPU

## Kurrichane Thrush  *Turdus libonyana*

**21–22 cm** A mostly brown thrush with *orange flanks*, white belly and vent, *orange eye-ring, orange-red bill* and *dark malar stripes*. Juv. similar to ad. but with black-brown spots to underparts. **Status and habitat:** Common resident in woodland, riparian forest and suburbia, particularly with open lawns to forage on. **SETSWANA: TSINTSIRU**

## Kalahari Scrub Robin
*Cercotrichas paena*

**14–16 cm** A sandy-brown scrub robin with *plain underparts, mostly plain upperparts*, pale supercilium, obvious dark eye-stripe, and *rufous rump and tail* with broad black subterminal band and white outer tail tips. Similar to White-browed Scrub Robin, but lacks malar stripes and white wing bars, and has plain (not streaked) underparts. **Status and habitat:** Very common resident in thornveld and dry woodland. **SETSWANA: PHÊNÊ**

## White-browed Scrub Robin
*Cercotrichas leucophrys*

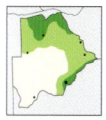

**14–16 cm** A light brown scrub robin with *obvious white wing bars, faintly dark-streaked pale underparts, dark malar stripes*, white supercilium with faint dark eye-stripe, rufous rump and uppertail with remainder of tail dark brown with white tips. Similar to plainer Kalahari Scrub Robin. **Status and habitat:** Common resident in savanna and woodland, particularly favouring thorn tree-dominated areas. **SETSWANA: PHÊNÊ**

### White-browed Robin-Chat
*Cossypha heuglini*

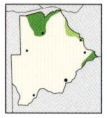

**18–19 cm** A mostly *bright orange* robin-chat with dark blue back and wings, and *black head with bold white supercilium*. In flight, dark tail with orange outer tail feathers obvious. A highly vocal species with a loud, repetitive song ending in a crescendo; regularly mimics other species. **Status and habitat:** Common resident in lush woodland, riparian forest, and suburbia.
**SETSWANA: RABOGALE**

### Fiscal Flycatcher   *Sigelus silens*

**18–20 cm** A distinctive *black-and-white flycatcher* with all-black crown, white wing bar, *thin bill*, and medium-length tail with *white outer tail feathers* (most obvious in flight). Similar to Southern Fiscal (p. 89), but lacks white scapular bar and supercilium, and has thin and sharp (not hooked) bill, and proportionately shorter tail. Female has grey-brown upperparts and grey-washed underparts. **Status and habitat:** Common localised resident in open shrubland and edges of savanna.
**SETSWANA: NAME UNKNOWN**

### Southern Black Flycatcher
*Melaenornis pammelaina*

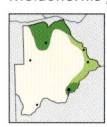

**18–20 cm** A medium-sized, *all-black flycatcher with square-ended tail* (may show slight notch), dark brown eyes, and weak bill. Similar to larger Fork-tailed Drongo (p. 91), but has square-ended tail, brown (not red) eyes, and slimmer bill. Confusion also possible with Black Cuckooshrike (p. 88), which has yellow gape and rounded tail. **Status and habitat:** Uncommon resident in woodland and edges of riparian forest. **SETSWANA: SE.ROTHÊ**

## Chat Flycatcher *Agricola infuscatus*

**20 cm** A heavyset brown flycatcher with very *little definition between upperparts and slightly paler underparts*, and *indistinct pale wing bar*. Similar to other brown flycatchers, such as Marico Flycatcher, which has contrasting plumage, Ashy Flycatcher (p. 118), and migratory Spotted Flycatcher. **Status and habitat:** Common resident of open country, including arid savanna and shrubland. SETSWANA: **KAPADINTSI**

## Marico Flycatcher
*Bradornis mariquensis*

**18 cm** A medium-sized flycatcher with *clear contrast between brown upperparts and white underparts*. Similar to Chat Flycatcher, Ashy Flycatcher (p. 118), and migratory Spotted Flycatcher, which has streaking on underparts and crown. **Status and habitat:** Common resident in arid savanna, particularly favouring acacia woodland. SETSWANA: **KAPADINTSI**

## Spotted Flycatcher *Muscicapa striata*

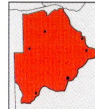

**13–14 cm** A small brown flycatcher with *diffusely streaked underparts, streaked crown* and long wings. Similar to Chat, Ashy (p. 118), and Marico flycatchers. **Status and habitat:** Common Palearctic-br. summer visitor occurring in open habitats, including savanna, woodland and suburbia. SETSWANA: **NAME UNKNOWN**

### Ashy Flycatcher  *Fraseria caerulescens*

**14–15 cm** A smallish *blue-grey flycatcher* with obvious *white eye-ring broken by dark eye-stripe*. Similar to other grey-brown flycatchers; smaller and greyer than Chat Flycatcher (p. 117), lacks distinct contrasting plumage of Marico Flycatcher (p. 117), and lacks spotted and streaked plumage of Spotted Flycatcher (p. 117). **Status and habitat:** Common resident in tall woodland and riparian forest. SETSWANA: NAME UNKNOWN

### African Paradise Flycatcher  *Terpsiphone viridis*

**20 cm (br. male 37 cm)** A *long-tailed flycatcher with chestnut upperparts and tail*, dark grey head, crest and chest, light grey underparts, and bright blue bill and eye-ring. Female lacks long tail and has dark bill. **Status and habitat:** Common intra-African br. summer visitor in woodland, riparian forest and suburbia. SETSWANA: KGOSI YADINÔNYANE

### African Stonechat  *Saxicola torquatus*

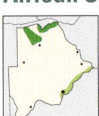

**13–14 cm** A small, strikingly patterned chat with *black head, dark rufous upper chest*, and *white neck patch*, wing bar, rump and lower belly. Female much plainer, with mottled brown head and pale cinnamon-orange underparts, and lacks white neck patch. **Status and habitat:** Common resident and partial migrant occurring in open habitats, including wetland edges, grassland, shrubland and agricultural land. SETSWANA: NAME UNKNOWN

## Ant-eating Chat
*Myrmecocichla formicivora*

**17–18 cm** A medium-sized, mostly *blackish-brown chat* with obvious *white wing patches* (visible only in flight), and indistinct *white shoulder patches*. Female lacks white shoulder patches. **Status and habitat:** Common resident in open habitats such as grassland and shrubland. SETSWANA: LE.PING

## Arnot's Chat
*Myrmecocichla arnotti*

**17–18 cm** A striking chat with *mostly black plumage and white crown and large shoulder patch*. Female with black crown, and white throat and upper chest. Juv. dull black, often showing white feathering on crown (male) or throat (female). **Status and habitat:** Common resident in tall, broadleaved woodland. SETSWANA: NAME UNKNOWN

## Capped Wheatear
*Oenanthe pileata*

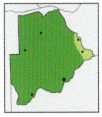

**17 cm** A striking wheatear with black cap, ear coverts and eye stripe, obvious *white supercilium* and *broad black breast band*. In flight, shows contrasting tail pattern with white uppertail and broad black tail tip in inverted V-shape. **Status and habitat:** Common resident and partial migrant occurring in open habitats such as semi-arid shrubland, dry grassland and fallow agricultural land. SETSWANA: NTIDI

### Collared Sunbird — *Hedydipna collaris*

**10–11 cm** A tiny *short-billed sunbird* with *iridescent green upperparts, head and throat, thin purple breast band* and bright yellow underparts. Female lacks green throat and purple breast band. Green-and-yellow coloration sets it apart from any other sunbird species in Botswana. **Status and habitat:** Common resident in lush woodland, riparian forest and suburbia. SETSWANA: SE.GÔKGÔ

### Amethyst Sunbird
*Chalcomitra amethystina*

**14–15 cm** A medium-sized, *mostly black sunbird with iridescent green forehead, and iridescent purple throat* and shoulder patch. Female has light grey upperparts, dark-streaked cream-white underparts, dark throat with pale malar stripe and thin pale supercilium. Female like female Scarlet-chested Sunbird, but has paler underparts, more obvious supercilium, and dark (not pale) shoulder edge. **Status and habitat:** Common resident in open woodland and suburbia. SETSWANA: SE.GÔKGÔ

### Scarlet-chested Sunbird
*Chalcomitra senegalensis*

**14 cm** A medium-sized, *mostly black sunbird with obvious bright scarlet chest,* and green throat and forehead. Female dark brown above, with dark-mottled and -streaked cream-grey underparts, pale shoulder edge and indistinct supercilium. Female similar to female Amethyst Sunbird. **Status and habitat:** Common resident in mixed habitats including open woodland and savanna and suburbia. SETSWANA: SE.GÔKGÔ

## Marico Sunbird  *Cinnyris mariquensis*

**12–13 cm** A small to medium-sized sunbird with *iridescent green back, head and breast, broad purple breast band*, dark belly, and a medium-length bill. Female grey-brown above with creamy underparts with heavy grey streaking. Female similar to female Dusky Sunbird. **Status and habitat:** Common resident in savanna, woodland, riparian forest and suburbia. SETSWANA: SE.GÔKGÔ

## White-bellied Sunbird  *Cinnyris talatala*

**11 cm** A small sunbird with *iridescent green back, head and breast, broad purple-blue breast band and bright white belly*. Female with plain grey-brown upperparts and plain or faintly streaked whitish-grey underparts. Female similar to female Dusky Sunbird, but ranges do not overlap; separated from other female sunbirds by much plainer underparts. **Status and habitat:** Common resident in savanna, woodland and suburbia. SETSWANA: SE.GÔKGÔ

## Dusky Sunbird  *Cinnyris fuscus*

**11–12 cm** A rather dull sunbird with *glossy black head, neck and mantle, dark throat and chest with bronzy iridescence*, and white belly. Non-br. male has plain grey upperparts and white underparts (with occasional dark breast feathers). Female like non-br. male, but lacks dark feathers to underparts. Female very similar to female White-bellied Sunbird, but ranges do not overlap, and female Marico Sunbird, but lacks any streaking to underparts. **Status and habitat:** Common resident in arid savanna and shrubland. SETSWANA: SE.GÔKGÔ

## Yellow-throated Bush Sparrow
*Gymnoris superciliaris*

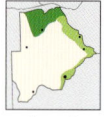

**15–16 cm** A woodland sparrow with *broad pale supercilium*, patterned brown upperparts, and paler underparts with *indistinct yellow throat patch* (not easily visible). Similar to female sparrows, but separated by obvious broad supercilium. **Status and habitat:** Common resident in broadleaved woodland and savanna. **SETSWANA: MMAMOJÊLA-RURE**

## Cape Sparrow
*Passer melanurus*

**15 cm** A strikingly marked sparrow with *black-and-white head, rich rufous upperparts* and whitish underparts. Female has light grey head with white supercilium and crescent on throat, and plain grey mantle. Female similar to female House and Great sparrows, but has plain grey (not streaked) mantle. **Status and habitat:** Common resident in open habitats, including grassland, semi-arid savanna and arid shrubland. **SETSWANA: THOROBÊ**

## Great Sparrow
*Passer motitensis*

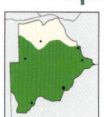

**15–16 cm** A heavy-billed sparrow with *rich rufous upperparts (including rump)*, grey crown and *small black bib*. Female has broad pale rufous supercilium and duller rufous back. Similar to House Sparrow, but has rufous (not grey) rump; male has smaller black bib and whitish lores; female has dull rufous (not pale) supercilium and chestnut (not greyish-brown) mantle; habitat preferences differ. **Status and habitat:** Common resident in semi-arid woodland and savanna. **SETSWANA: TSWERE**

## Southern Grey-headed Sparrow
*Passer diffusus*

**15 cm** A grey-and-chestnut sparrow with an all-grey head and *breast*, black bill, *chestnut shoulders and rump, and small white wing bar.* Non-br. ad. has horn-coloured bill. Easily separated from other sparrow species by complete lack of supercilium or any obvious patterning. **Status and habitat:** Common and widespread resident in savanna, woodland and around rural settlements.
SETSWANA: **MMAMOJÊLA-RURE**

## House Sparrow          *Passer domesticus*

**14–15 cm** A distinctive-looking sparrow with *large black bib extending onto chest, grey crown and rump*, and buffy brown back. Female lacks black bib and has duller greyish-brown patterned back with indistinct pale supercilium. Both sexes like Great Sparrow; female similar to female Cape Sparrow, but has patterned (not plain) mantle and drabber greyish-brown (not rufous) upperparts. **Status and habitat:** Common introduced resident in human-modified habitats, including cities, towns and rural settlements. SETSWANA: **TSWERE**

## Red-billed Buffalo Weaver
*Bubalornis niger*

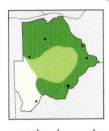

**22–23 cm** A large *black weaver with red bill, and white mottling to upper flanks.* Female is mostly blackish-brown with faintly scaled underparts and a duller red bill. White wing panel in both sexes most obvious in flight. Nests in large, untidy colonial stick nests with up to eight nest chambers. **Status and habitat:** Common resident in savanna and woodland.
SETSWANA: **POÊNYANE**

## White-browed Sparrow-Weaver
*Plocepasser mahali*

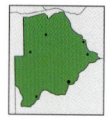

**17 cm** A brown-and-white weaver with *obvious white supercilium*, brown upperparts with pale wing bars, black bill, and *clean white rump* (most obvious in flight). Female like male, but with slightly paler bill. Nests in small, untidy grass nests, often with many nests in a single tree. **Status and habitat:** Very common and widespread resident in semi-arid savanna and woodland. **SETSWANA: MO.GALÊ**

## Thick-billed Weaver
*Amblyospiza albifrons*

**18 cm** A large, strikingly marked *dark brown weaver* with *heavy black bill, clear white forehead and small white wing patch*. Female dull brown (lacking white forehead and wing patches), with horn-coloured bill, and heavily streaked pale underparts. **Status and habitat:** Common resident in reed beds on wetland edges; feeds in neighbouring woodland and riparian forest in non-br. season. **SETSWANA: POÊNYANE**

## Sociable Weaver   *Philetairus socius*

**14 cm** A smallish tan brown weaver with *black bib*, heavy grey bill, brown crown, and *scaled flanks and nape*. Highly gregarious, with hundreds of birds nesting and roosting in a single huge straw nest, which is often simultaneously used by other bird species, including predatory Pygmy Falcon (p. 40). **Status and habitat:** Common resident and local nomad in arid and semi-arid savanna; needs large trees or utility poles to build nests. **SETSWANA: KGWÊRÊRÊ**

## Scaly-feathered Weaver
*Sporopipes squamifrons*

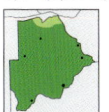

**10–11 cm** A very small, pale, finch-like weaver with *finely scaled crown*, strongly scaled wing coverts, *pink bill and obvious black malar stripes*. In flight, white outer tail feathers are evident. **Status and habitat:** Common and widespread resident and local nomad in arid and semi-arid acacia savanna.
**SETSWANA: LE.TSETSENKANA**

## Holub's Golden Weaver
*Ploceus xanthops*

**17 cm** A rather large, heavy set, *bright yellow weaver* with yellow-green upperparts, *pale eyes* and *heavy black bill*. Female drabber yellow with darker upperparts. Female similar to other female weavers, but fairly uniformly yellow, with heavy black bill and pale eyes. **Status and habitat:** A locally common resident in woodland and riparian forest. **SETSWANA: TALÊ**

## Lesser Masked Weaver
*Ploceus intermedius*

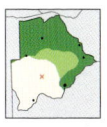

**13–14 cm** A small yellow weaver with *large black mask (encompassing forehead and crown), pale eyes, greyish legs* and delicate bill. Non-br. male and female dull yellow and lack black mask. Both sexes similar to Southern Masked and Village weavers (p. 126); br. male separated by black mask covering forehead and crown, and pale eyes; non-br. male and female separated by small size, pale eyes and grey legs. **Status and habitat:** Common to uncommon resident of savanna, woodland and edges of rivers and swamps. **SETSWANA: THAGA**

### Southern Masked Weaver
*Ploceus velatus*

**15–16 cm** A medium-sized yellow weaver with *black mask (marginally extending onto forehead)*, pink-red legs, *bright red eyes* and stout bill. Non-br. male and female mostly dull brown, lacking mask, with dark eyes. Like Lesser Masked (p. 125) and Village weavers; male separated by black mask extending onto forehead, and red eyes; non-br. male and female separated by dark eyes, reddish legs and stout bill. **Status and habitat:** Common resident in wooded habitats and agricultural land. **SETSWANA: THAGA**

### Village Weaver
*Ploceus cucullatus*

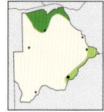

**16 cm** A medium-sized yellow weaver with *all-black head* (southern subsp. *spilonotus* has full yellow crown), *mottled mantle*, red eye, reddish legs, and *longish, heavy bill*. Non-br. male and female have dull yellow underparts and red-brown eyes, and lack mask. Like Lesser (p. 125) and Southern masked weavers but male has all-black head and mottled mantle; non-br. male and female larger, with longer heavier bill, red-brown eyes and reddish legs. **Status and habitat:** Common resident in savanna, woodland and suburbia. **SETSWANA: THAGA**

### Red-headed Weaver
*Anaplectes rubriceps*

**14–15 cm** A striking *red-headed weaver with red mantle and breast*, orange-red bill, clean white belly, and olive-brown wings with dull yellow wing panel. Non-br. male and female have dull yellow head and breast, and more orange bill. Female similar to other female weavers, but separated by orange bill and dull yellow wing panel. **Status and habitat:** Common resident in savanna and woodland. **SETSWANA: THAGA**

QUELEA, BISHOPS 127

## Red-billed Quelea  *Quelea quelea*

**12 cm** A small weaver-like bird with *heavy, bright red bill*, faint red eye-ring, and variably coloured head: most have *black face mask with pink or buff crown and breast*; some have indistinct cream-white mask. Non-br. male and female dull grey-brown with streaked mantle and orange-red bill. *Highly gregarious*, often found in massive flocks numbering into the millions. **Status and habitat:** Common resident and nomad found in savanna, grassland and agricultural land. SETSWANA: **THAGA**

## Southern Red Bishop  *Euplectes orix*

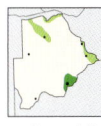

**12–13 cm** A conspicuous red-and-black bishop with *red upperparts and collar, and black lower breast, belly and facial mask*. Non-br. male and female light brown with streaked chest and upperparts, and dull yellow supercilium. Almost identical to non-br. male or female Yellow-crowned Bishop, but with heavier and more evenly streaked underparts, including belly; best identified by presence of striking br. male. **Status and habitat:** Common resident in reed beds, grassland, and agricultural land; normally near water. SETSWANA: **THAGA**

## Yellow-crowned Bishop
*Euplectes afer*

**10–11 cm** A small, strikingly coloured yellow-and-black bishop, w*ith bright yellow crown, lower back and rump*; reminiscent of large bumblebee in display flight. Non-br. male and female light brown with lightly streaked underparts and mostly plain white belly. Almost identical to non-br. male or female Southern Red Bishop; best identified by presence of striking br. male. **Status and habitat:** Common resident in marshes and floodplains; moves to drier areas, including agricultural land, in non-br. season.
SETSWANA: **THAGA**

### Fan-tailed Widowbird
*Euplectes axillaris*

**15 cm** A *mostly black bird with broad, medium-length tail, rufous-red shoulder patches* and light grey bill. Non-br. male and female mostly light brown with small dull orange shoulder patch (often obscured), heavily marked mantle, dark wing coverts, finely streaked pale underparts and pinkish bill. Very similar to female Southern Red and Yellow-crowned bishops (p. 127), but best separated by dull orange shoulder patch. **Status and habitat:** Common resident in reed beds and swamps. **SETSWANA: MO.LOPE**

### Pin-tailed Whydah     *Vidua macroura*

**12 cm (br. male 26-34 cm)** A striking *black-and-white whydah with fine, long black tail,* bright red bill and dark legs. Non-br. male and female mostly brown, with short tail, boldly striped head, pale tips to outer tail, and dark (female only) bill. Similar to non-br. male or female Shaft-tailed Whydah, best separated by dark (not red) legs. Brood parasite of Common Waxbill (p. 130). **Status and habitat:** Common resident in a variety of open habitats, including grassland, savanna, agricultural land and suburbia. **SETSWANA: MO.LOPE**

### Shaft-tailed Whydah     *Vidua regia*

**11 cm (br. male 28–34 cm)** Unmistakable whydah with *long, wispy tail with spatulate tips,* dull orange underparts and hind collar, black upperparts, crown and face, and red bill and legs. Non-br. male and female mostly brown, with striped head and pale tips to outer tail. Similar to non-br. male or female Pin-tailed Whydah. Brood parasite of Violet-eared Waxbill (p. 131) and other waxbill species. **Status and habitat:** Common resident in semi-arid savanna and woodland. **SETSWANA: MO.LOPE**

## Long-tailed Paradise Whydah
*Vidua paradisaea*

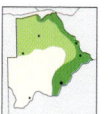

**16 cm (br. male 36 cm)** A distinctive whydah with *broad-based, long wispy tail*, black upperparts, crown and mask, *buff orange hind collar and belly*, and broad rufous breast band. Non-br. male and female mostly brown with black-and-white striped head, with dark 'C' mark on ear coverts. Separated from other female whydahs by dark ear coverts, and bill and leg colour. Brood parasite of Green-winged Pytilia (p. 132). **Status and habitat:** Common resident and local nomad in savanna and woodland. **SETSWANA: MO.LOPE**

## Village Indigobird
*Vidua chalybeata*

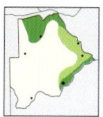

**11 cm** A small, *glossy black, red-legged bird*, which occurs as two subspecies: *white-billed* in the northwest and *red-billed* in the southeast. Non-br. male and female are dull brown with brown-and-white striped head; bill colour varies according to subspecies. Very similar to female Shaft-tailed Whydah, but has more boldly marked head and evenly coloured tail tip. Brood parasite of Red-billed (p. 131) and Brown (p. 132) firefinches. **Status and habitat:** Common resident in savanna, woodland and agricultural land. **SETSWANA: NAME UNKNOWN**

## Red-headed Finch
*Amadina erythrocephala*

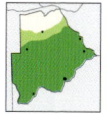

**14 cm** A plump, *red-headed finch* with pale conical-shaped bill, *intricate white spots (with dark outlines) on underparts* and white tip to tail. Female has plain brown head, with slight rufous wash to nape and hind crown, and heavily barred throat with faintly spotted belly. Similar to female Cut-throat Finch, but has plain (not barred) red-brown crown and nape. **Status and habitat:** Common resident and nomad in arid and semi-arid grassland, savanna and shrubland. **SETSWANA: NTSETSE**

### Cut-throat Finch      *Amadina fasciata*

**12 cm** A small finch with *crimson red throat band, densely barred crown and nape, and heavily scaled underparts* with tawny-brown patch on lower belly (not easily visible). Female similar to male but lacks red throat band. Similar to female Red-headed Finch (p. 129). **Status and habitat:** Uncommon resident in woodland and savanna.
**SETSWANA: NTSETSE**

### Common Waxbill      *Estrilda astrild*

**11–12 cm** A brown waxbill with *faint uniformly barred upper- and underparts*, plain grey throat, *red bill and eye-stripe*, and black lower belly and vent. Female slightly paler than male. **Status and habitat:** Common resident in lush vegetation in savanna and grassland, particularly favouring tall grass and reeds, mostly near water. **SETSWANA: RAMOTSIISANÊNG**

### Black-faced Waxbill
*Brunhilda erythronotos*

**12–13 cm** A dark grey waxbill with *black face mask, deep crimson lower chest, belly and rump*, and densely barred grey wings. Female similar to male but slightly paler. **Status and habitat:** Common resident in arid and semi-arid savanna, particularly favouring acacia savanna, as well as heavily vegetated riparian bush. **SETSWANA: LE.BIIBII**

## Violet-eared Waxbill
*Granatina granatina*

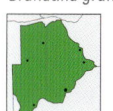

**13–14 cm** A colourful waxbill with mostly *chestnut plumage, purple cheek patches, red bill*, blue forehead and rump, and *longish black tail*. Female similar to male, but with dull brown upperparts and fawn underparts. **Status and habitat:** Common resident in savanna and dry woodland, favouring acacia thickets. **SETSWANA: RALETSÔKU**

## Blue Waxbill    *Uraeginthus angolensis*

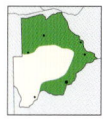

**12–13 cm** A small waxbill with *light blue face, underparts and tail*, light brown crown, back and wings, and dark bill. Female slightly duller blue than male. Juv. has blue restricted to breast and face. A vocal species giving high-pitched, wispy '*sreee*' notes. **Status and habitat:** Common resident in woodland and savanna. **SETSWANA: LE.BIIBII**

## Red-billed Firefinch
*Lagonosticta senegala*

**10 cm** A small *pink-red* firefinch with *red bill*, prominent *cream-yellow eye-ring*, bright red rump, small white spots on sides of breast, and *light brown vent*, lower belly, back and wings. Female mostly brown with pink-red restricted to bill, lores, rump and tail, and with extensive white spotting on sides of breast. Male similar to Jameson's Firefinch (p. 132); female similar to Brown Firefinch (p. 132). **Status and habitat:** Common resident in savanna, woodland and suburbia. **SETSWANA: NTSETSE**

### Jameson's Firefinch
*Lagonosticta rhodopareia*

**11 cm** A mostly pink-red firefinch with *black bill*, white spots on sides of breast, *red rump and tail, dark vent*, and brown wings. Female buff-red with paler brown upperparts and brown crown. Male separated from male Red-billed (p. 131) and Brown firefinches by black bill and vent; female separated from female Red-billed and Brown firefinches by brighter underparts and black bill. **Status and habitat:** Common to uncommon resident in savanna and woodland.
**SETSWANA: NTSETSE**

### Brown Firefinch   *Lagonosticta nitidula*

**10 cm** A greyish-brown firefinch with *purple-red bill, dull red face and breast* (with white spots on sides of breast), *and brown rump and tail*. Female is duller with dull red restricted to lores and throat. Similar to Jameson's and female Red-billed firefinches (p. 131), but has brown (not red) rump and tail and lacks creamy eye-ring. **Status and habitat:** Common localised resident of marshes, reed beds and scrub near water, as well as riparian woodland.
**SETSWANA: NTSETSE**

### Green-winged Pytilia   *Pytilia melba*

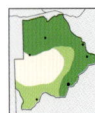

**13 cm** A brightly coloured finch with *green back, wings and chest*, grey ear coverts and nape, *red crown, throat and tail*, and *grey-and-white-barred underparts*. Female has grey crown, throat and breast. Separated from other finch species by bright coloration and barred underparts. **Status and habitat:** Common resident in thickets within savanna and woodland. **SETSWANA: NAME UNKNOWN**

## Black-throated Canary
*Crithagra atrogularis*

**11–12 cm** A rather *dull grey-brown canary* with *variable black throat patch*, faint or heavily streaked underparts and *bright yellow rump*. Female often with reduced black throat. In flight, *pale-tipped tail* is evident. Similar to female Yellow Canary, but has bright yellow (not dull olive) rump and pale-tipped tail, and lacks strong malar stripe and olive wing margins. **Status and habitat:** Common resident in savanna, dry woodland and suburbia. SETSWANA: **MO.RAGANE**

## Yellow-fronted Canary
*Crithagra mozambica*

**11–12 cm** A mostly yellow canary with *boldly marked face (yellow supercilium, grey ear coverts and crown, and dark malar stripe)*, variably marked olive upperparts and yellow underparts. In flight, *pale-tipped tail and yellow rump* evident. Similar to female Yellow Canary, but separated by yellow underparts and rump, and pale-tipped tail. **Status and habitat:** Common resident in savanna, woodland, riparian forest and suburbia. SETSWANA: **MO.RAGANE**

## Yellow Canary *Crithagra flaviventris*

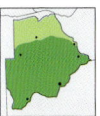

**13–14 cm** A *bright yellow* canary with *boldly marked face (yellow supercilium, dull olive ear coverts, and dark malar stripe)*, slightly darker upperparts and yellow rump. Female much duller, with pale supercilium and underparts, and dull olive wing margins and rump. Similar to Black-throated and Yellow-fronted canaries. **Status and habitat:** Common resident in semi-arid shrubland and savanna. SETSWANA: **MO.RAGANE**

### Lark-like Bunting  Emberiza impetuani

**14 cm** A *plainly marked* all-brown bunting with *pale supercilium, faint malar stripe,* and chestnut-brown wing panel. Similar to various lark species; separated by smaller size and small, conical bill. **Status and habitat:** Common resident and nomad occurring erratically across Botswana and prone to irruptions. Found in arid and semi-arid shrubland and grassland. SETSWANA: NAME UNKNOWN

### Cinnamon-breasted Bunting
Emberiza tahapisi

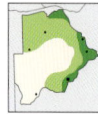

**14–15 cm** A dark bunting with *black-and-white-striped head*, black upper breast, *chestnut underparts,* pale-edged feathering to mottled brown upperparts, and yellow lower mandible. Female has duller grey-black head and upper breast. **Status and habitat:** Common resident and local nomad in rocky woodland and grassland. SETSWANA: KWABEBE

### Golden-breasted Bunting
Emberiza flaviventris

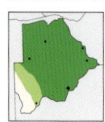

**15–16 cm** A striking bunting with *bold black-and-white striped head*, chestnut brown upperparts, and *yellow underparts with golden breast.* In flight, white outer tail feathers obvious. Female is very similar, with less boldly marked head. **Status and habitat:** Common resident in savanna, woodland and shrubland. SETSWANA: THAGAPITSE

# INDEX TO SCIENTIFIC NAMES

## A

*Accipiter ovampensis* 38
*Acridotheres tristis* 111
*Acrocephalus gracilirostris* 103
   *scirpaceus* 104
*Actitis hypoleucos* 56
*Actophilornis africanus* 49
*Afrotis afraoides* 47
*Agricola infuscatus* 117
*Alopochen aegyptiaca* 27
*Amadina erythrocephala* 129
   *fasciata* 130
*Amblyospiza albifrons* 124
*Anaplectes rubriceps* 126
*Anarhynchus asiaticus* 53
   *pallidus* 53
   *pecuarius* 54
*Anas capensis* 29
   *erythrorhyncha* 29
   *undulata* 29
*Anastomus lamelligerus* 22
*Anhinga rufa* 24
*Anthoscopus minutus* 93
*Anthus cinnamomeus* 97
   *vaalensis* 97
*Apalis flavida* 108
*Apus affinis* 73
   *apus* 73
   *caffer* 73
*Aquila rapax* 33
   *spilogaster* 35
*Ardea alba* 21
   *brachyrhyncha* 21
   *cinerea* 18
   *goliath* 19
   *ibis* 22
   *melanocephala* 19
   *purpurea* 19
*Ardeola ralloides* 18
   *rufiventris* 20
*Ardeotis kori* 46
*Asio capensis* 70

## B

*Batis molitor* 84
   *pririt* 85
*Bostrychia hagedash* 15
*Botaurus sturmii* 17

*Bradornis mariquensis* 117
*Bradypterus baboecala* 103
*Brunhilda erythronotos* 130
*Bubalornis niger* 123
*Bubo africanus* 70
*Bucorvus leadbeateri* 75
*Buphagus africanus* 114
   *erythrorynchus* 114
*Burhinus capensis* 50
   *vermiculatus* 50
*Buteo buteo* 37
*Butorides striata* 18

## C

*Calamonastes fasciolatus* 108
*Calandrella cinerea* 96
*Calendulauda africanoides* 95
   *sabota* 94
*Calherodius leuconotus* 17
*Calidris ferruginea* 55
   *minuta* 56
   *pugnax* 55
*Camaroptera brevicaudata* 108
*Campephaga flava* 88
*Campethera abingoni* 83
   *bennettii* 83
*Campocolinus coqui* 43
*Caprimulgus fossii* 72
   *pectoralis* 72
   *rufigena* 71
*Cecropis abyssinica* 102
   *cucullata* 102
   *semirufa* 102
*Centropus cupreicaudus* 67
   *grillii* 68
   *senegalensis* 67
   *superciliosus* 68
*Cercotrichas leucophrys* 115
   *paena* 115
*Certhilauda chuana* 96
*Ceryle rudis* 78
*Chalcomitra amethystina* 120
   *senegalensis* 120
*Charadrius hiaticula* 53
   *tricollaris* 54
*Chersomanes albofasciata* 94
*Chlidonias hybrida* 59
   *leucopterus* 60

*Chlorocichla flaviventris* 99
*Chlorophoneus sulfureopectus* 85
*Chloropicus namaquus* 84
*Chroicocephalus cirrocephalus* 59
*Chrysococcyx caprius* 66
   *klaas* 67
*Ciconia abdimii* 23
   *ciconia* 23
   *microscelis* 24
*Cinnyricinclus leucogaster* 113
*Cinnyris fuscus* 121
   *mariquensis* 121
   *talatala* 121
*Circaetus cinereus* 35
   *pectoralis* 35
*Circus ranivorus* 36
*Cisticola aridulus* 106
   *chiniana* 105
   *fulvicapilla* 106
   *juncidis* 106
   *pipiens* 105
   *rufilatus* 105
*Clamator glandarius* 65
   *jacobinus* 65
   *levaillantii* 65
*Clanga pomarina* 34
*Columba guinea* 61
   *livia* 61
*Coracias caudatus* 77
   *garrulus* 77
   *naevius* 77
*Corvus albus* 92
   *capensis* 91
*Corypha africana* 96
   *asciolata* 95
*Corythornis cristatus* 79
*Cossypha heuglini* 116
*Coturnix delegorguei* 44
*Creatophora cinerea* 111
*Crecopsis egregia* 49
*Crinifer concolor* 64
*Crithagra atrogularis* 133
   *flaviventris* 133
   *mozambica* 133
*Cuculus clamosus* 66
   *gularis* 66
*Curruca subcoerulea* 109
*Cursorius temminckii* 57
*Cypsiurus parvus* 72

## D
*Delichon urbicum* 100
*Dendrocygna bicolor* 26
   *viduata* 26
*Dendropicos fuscescens* 84
*Dicrurus adsimilis* 91
*Dryoscopus cubla* 86

## E
*Egretta ardesiaca* 20
   *garzetta* 21
   *vinaceigula* 20
*Elanus caeruleus* 39
*Emberiza flaviventris* 134
   *impetuani* 134
   *tahapisi* 134
*Ephippiorhynchus senegalensis* 24
*Eremomela icteropygialis* 109
   *usticollis* 109
*Eremopterix leucotis* 93
   *verticalis* 93
*Estrilda astrild* 130
*Euplectes afer* 127
   *axillaris* 128
   *orix* 127
*Eurocephalus anguitimens* 88
*Eurystomus glaucurus* 78

## F
*Falco biarmicus* 41
   *chicquera* 41
   *dickinsoni* 41
   *rupicoloides* 40
   *rupicolus* 40
   *subbuteo* 42
*Fraseria caerulescens* 118
*Fulica cristata* 47

## G
*Gallinago nigripennis* 55
*Gallinula chloropus* 48
*Glareola pratincola* 58
*Glaucidium capense* 69
   *perlatum* 69
*Granatina granatina* 131
*Grus carunculata* 45
*Gymnoris superciliaris* 122
*Gyps africanus* 31
   *coprotheres* 31

## H

*Halcyon chelicuti* 79
   *senegalensis* 79
*Hedydipna collaris* 120
*Hieraaetus pennatus* 34
   *wahlbergi* 34
*Himantopus himantopus* 51
*Hippolais icterina* 104
*Hirundo dimidiata* 101
   *rustica* 101
   *smithii* 101

## I

*Icthyophaga vocifer* 32
*Indicator indicator* 83

## K

*Kaupifalco monogrammicus* 39
*Ketupa lactea* 71

## L

*Lagonosticta nitidula* 132
   *rhodopareia* 132
   *senegala* 131
*Lamprotornis australis* 113
   *chalybaeus* 112
   *mevesii* 112
   *nitens* 112
*Laniarius atrococcineus* 87
   *bicolor* 86
*Lanius collaris* 89
   *collurio* 90
   *melanoleucus* 89
   *minor* 89
*Leptoptilos crumenifer* 22
*Lissotis melanogaster* 46
*Lophoceros bradfieldi* 76
   *nasutus* 76
*Lophotis ruficrista* 46
*Lybius torquatus* 82

## M

*Malcorus pectoralis* 107
*Megaceryle maxima* 78
*Melaenornis pammelaina* 116
*Melaniparus cinerascens* 92
   *niger* 92
*Melierax canorus* 37
   *metabates* 37
*Merops apiaster* 81
   *bullockoides* 80
   *hirundineus* 80
   *nubicoides* 81
   *persicus* 81
   *pusillus* 80
*Microcarbo africanus* 25
*Micronisus gabar* 38
*Microparra capensis* 50
*Milvus aegyptius* 36
*Mirafra passerina* 95
*Motacilla aguimp* 98
   *capensis* 97
*Muscicapa striata* 117
*Mycteria ibis* 23
*Myrmecocichla arnotti* 119
   *formicivora* 119

## N

*Necrosyrtes monachus* 30
*Neophedina cincta* 99
*Netta erythrophthalma* 30
*Nettapus auritus* 28
*Nilaus afer* 87
*Numida meleagris* 42
*Nycticorax nycticorax* 17

## O

*Oena capensis* 63
*Oenanthe pileata* 119
*Onychognathus morio* 113
*Oriolus auratus* 90
   *larvatus* 91
   *oriolus* 90
*Ortygornis sephaena* 42
*Otus senegalensis* 69
*Oxyura maccoa* 30

## P

*Paragallinula angulata* 48
*Passer diffusus* 123
   *domesticus* 123
   *melanurus* 122
   *motitensis* 122
*Pelecanus onocrotalus* 14
   *rufescens* 14
*Phalacrocorax lucidus* 25
*Philetairus socius* 124
*Phoeniconaias minor* 16
*Phoenicopterus roseus* 16
*Phoeniculus purpureus* 74
*Phyllastrephus terrestris* 99
*Phylloscopus trochilus* 104
*Pinarocorys nigricans* 94
*Platalea alba* 14

*Plectropterus gambensis* 27
*Plegadis falcinellus* 15
*Plocepasser mahali* 124
*Ploceus cucullatus* 126
   *intermedius* 125
   *velatus* 126
   *xanthops* 125
*Poicephalus meyeri* 64
*Polemaetus bellicosus* 33
*Polihierax semitorquatus* 40
*Polyboroides typus* 36
*Porphyrio alleni* 48
   *madagascariensis* 47
*Prinia flavicans* 107
   *subflava* 107
*Prionops plumatus* 87
   *retzii* 88
*Pternistis adspersus* 43
   *natalensis* 44
   *swainsonii* 44
*Pterocles bicinctus* 60
   *burchelli* 61
   *namaqua* 60
*Ptilopsis granti* 70
*Pycnonotus nigricans* 98
   *tricolor* 98
*Pytilia melba* 132

## Q
*Quelea quelea* 127

## R
*Recurvirostra avosetta* 51
*Rhinopomastus cyanomelas* 75
*Rhinoptilus africanus* 58
   *chalcopterus* 58
*Riparia paludicola* 100
   *riparia* 100
*Rostratula benghalensis* 54
*Rynchops flavirostris* 59

## S
*Sagittarius serpentarius* 32
*Sarkidiornis melanotos* 27
*Saxicola torquatus* 118
*Scleroptila gutturalis* 43
*Scopus umbretta* 16
*Scotopelia peli* 71
*Sigelus silens* 116
*Spatula hottentota* 28
   *smithii* 28
*Spilopelia senegalensis* 63
*Sporopipes squamifrons* 125

*Streptopelia capicola* 62
   *decipiens* 62
   *semitorquata* 62
*Struthio camelus* 45
*Sylvietta rufescens* 103

## T
*Tachybaptus ruficollis* 25
*Tachyspiza badia* 38
   *minulla* 39
*Tchagra australis* 86
   *senegalus* 85
*Terathopius ecaudatus* 33
*Terpsiphone viridis* 118
*Thalassornis leuconotus* 26
*Threskiornis aethiopicus* 15
*Tockus leucomelas* 76
   *rufirostris* 75
*Torgos tracheliotos* 31
*Trachyphonus vaillantii* 82
*Treron calvus* 64
*Tricholaema leucomelas* 82
*Trigonoceps occipitalis* 32
*Tringa glareola* 56
   *nebularia* 57
   *stagnatilis* 57
*Turdoides bicolor* 110
   *hartlaubii* 111
   *jardineii* 110
*Turdus libonyana* 115
   *litsitsirupa* 114
*Turnix sylvaticus* 45
*Turtur chalcospilos* 63
*Tyto alba* 68

## U
*Upupa africana* 74
*Uraeginthus angolensis* 131
*Urocolius indicus* 74

## V
*Vanellus armatus* 52
   *coronatus* 52
   *crassirostris* 51
   *senegallus* 52
*Vidua chalybeata* 129
   *macroura* 128
   *paradisaea* 129
   *regia* 128

## Z
*Zapornia flavirostra* 49
*Zosterops anderssoni* 110

# INDEX TO SETSWANA NAMES

## B
Bibing 31

## G
Ghubê 22

## H
Hêgha 64

## J
Jôkôsekêi 84, 85

## K
Kala 114
Kapadintsi 117
Kedikilê 43
Kelema-kele-nôsi 97
Kgaka 42
Kgapu 17
Kgaragoba 87
Kgoadira 32
Kgokgonoka 47, 48
Kgôri 46
Kgosi yadinônyane 118
Kgwadi 44
Kgwarakgwêtlhane 103, 104
Kgwêrêrê 124
Kôkôlôfutê 19
Kôkôlôhutwe 15
Kokomore 83, 84
Kôkôpa 82
Kokwana yanoka 49
Kopaopê 82
Kôrwê 75, 76
Kukuruma 70
Kwabebe 134

## L
Le.biibii 130, 131
Le.eba 61, 62, 64
Le.ebaroba 61
Le.fututu 67, 68
Le.gakabê 91, 92
Le.gôdi 112, 113
Le.gwaragwara 60, 61
Le.harathata 27
Le.hututu 75
Le.kôllwane 23, 24
Le.kôlôlwane 22, 23
Le.nkutshwêu 88
Le.nông 31
Le.phôi 62
Le.phurrwana 45, 50
Le.ping 119
Le.ranthata 87
Le.rweerwee 52
Le.sogo 43
Le.thulatshipi 52
Le.tlêrêtlêrê 77, 78
Le.tlhapêlapula 58
Le.tsetsenkana 125
Le.tshêga-nôga 74
Le.tshêganôga 110, 111
Le.tsiababa 74
Le.tsiêkwane 42, 43
Le.tsôbu 71
Le.tsukwê 27
Le.tsutsurôpu 114
Le.wewe 26
Le.wiiwii 26
Le.ya 14
Letsôpi 113

## M
Makokwe 66
Maritinkolê 98, 99
Mmadilêpê 74
Mmaleswana 14
Mmamasiloanoka 16
Mmamathêbê 47, 48
Mmamojêla-rure 122, 123
Mmamoleane 21
Mmamphuphama 72
Mmankgôdi 36, 37
Mmankgôtlhô 70, 71
Mmankgôtlhwê 69
Mo.galê 124
Mo.gatsa-kwêna 49
Mo.gôlôdi 45
Mo.gôlôri 16, 21
Mo.kgwêba 46
Mo.koe 64
Mo.kudunyane 63
Mo.leane 21, 22
Mo.lômbwe 24
Mo.lope 128, 129

Mo.ngwangwa 50
Mo.ragane 133
Mo.rôkapula 65
Mo.rubisana 69
Mo.rubise 70
Mo.salakatane 56, 57, 97, 98
Morôkapula 81
Motlhanka-wamanông 30, 32
Mpshe 45

## N

Nônyane 65
Nônyane yapula 95
Nqumu 71
Ntidi 119
Ntsetse 129, 130, 131, 132
Ntsu 33, 34, 35

## P

Para-lanku 109
Pêolane 72, 73, 99, 100, 101, 102
Pêtlêkê 33
Phakalane 39, 40, 41
Phakwe 41
Phênakgômo 85, 86
Phênê 115
Poênyane 123, 124
Pônyane 111
Poponaka 103

## Q

Qoqonamuti 83

## R

Rabogale 116
Raletsôku 131
Ramolôngwana 32
Ramotsiisanêng 130
Rankô 27
Rankudinyane 63
Reole 113

## S

Sasoo 86
Se.bataledi 92
Se.bota 94, 95, 96
Se.botêkgômo 96
Se.fudi 26, 28, 29
Se.gôdi 35, 36
Se.gôkgô 120, 121
Se.golagola 57, 58
Se.gôôtsane 36, 37, 38
Se.gwêba 44
Se.hudi 26, 28, 29, 30
Se.hudi sêsefatshwa 27
Se.hutsana 28
Se.inwêdi 78, 79
Se.kea 68
Se.khuko 20
Se.khwiri 44
Se.kopamarumo 69
Se.ngwêpê 18
Se.nwêdi 25
Se.rothê 91, 116
Se.sêlamarumô 80
Se.setlo 93
Sebôdu 75

## T

Talê 125
Thaga 125, 126, 127
Thagapitse 134
Thatswane 54
Thatswane wadikubu 51
Thorobê 122
Tilodi 89
Timêlêtsane 24, 25
Tlatlawê 47
Tlêntlêrêhuu 86
Tlhôlabaêng 82
Tlhômêdi 89
Tôntôbane 107
Tôntôsi 105, 106
Tshababarwa 15
Tshêtlho 83
Tshilwane 93
Tsintsiru 115
Tsôkwane 63
Tswere 122, 123

# INDEX TO COMMON NAMES

## A
Apalis, Yellow-breasted 108
Avocet, Pied 51

## B
Babbler, Arrow-marked 110
　Hartlaub's 111
　Southern Pied 110
Barbet, Acacia Pied 82
　Black-collared 82
　Crested 82
Bateleur 33
Batis, Chinspot 84
　Pririt 85
Bee-eater, Blue-cheeked 81
　European 81
　Little 80
　Southern Carmine 81
　Swallow-tailed 80
　White-fronted 80
Bishop, Southern Red 127
　Yellow-crowned 127
Bittern, Dwarf 17
Boubou, Swamp 86
Brownbul, Terrestrial 99
Brubru 87
Bulbul, African Red-eyed 98
　Dark-capped 98
Bunting, Cinnamon-breasted 134
　Golden-breasted 134
　Lark-like 134
Bushshrike, Orange-breasted 85
Bustard, Black-bellied 46
　Kori 46
Buttonquail, Common 45
Buzzard, Common 37
　Lizard 39

## C
Camaroptera, Grey-backed 108
Canary, Black-throated 133
　Yellow-fronted 133
　Yellow 133
Chat, Ant-eating 119
　Arnot's 119
Cisticola, Chirping 105
　Desert 106
　Rattling 105
　Tinkling 105
　Zitting 106
Coot, Red-knobbed 47
Cormorant, Reed 25
　White-breasted 25
Coucal, Black 68
　Coppery-tailed 67
　Senegal 67
　White-browed 68
Courser, Bronze-winged 58
　Double-banded 58
　Temminck's 57
Crake, African 49
　Black 49
Crane, Wattled 45
Crombec, Long-billed 103
Crow, Cape 91
　Pied 92
Cuckoo, African 66
　Black 66
　Diederik 66
　Great Spotted 65
　Jacobin 65
　Klaas's 67
　Levaillant's 65
Cuckooshrike, Black 88

## D
Darter, African 24
Dove, Emerald-spotted Wood 63
　Laughing 63
　Mourning Collared 62
　Namaqua 63
　Red-eyed 62
　Ring-necked 62
　Rock 61
Drongo, Fork-tailed 91
Duck, Fulvous Whistling 26
　Knob-billed 27
　Maccoa 30
　White-backed 26
　White-faced Whistling 26
　Yellow-billed 29

## E
Eagle, African Fish 32
　Black-chested Snake 35
　Booted 34

Brown Snake 35
Lesser Spotted 34
Martial 33
Tawny 33
Wahlberg's 34
Eagle-Owl, Spotted 70
Verreaux's 71
Egret, Great 21
Little 21
Medium 21
Slaty 20
Western Cattle 22
Eremomela, Burnt-necked 109
Yellow-bellied 109

## F
Falcon, Lanner 41
Pygmy 40
Red-necked 41
Finch, Cut-throat 130
Red-headed 129
Firefinch, Brown 132
Jameson's 132
Red-billed 131
Fiscal, Southern 89
Flamingo, Greater 16
Lesser 16
Flycatcher, African Paradise 118
Ashy 118
Chat 117
Fiscal 116
Marico 117
Southern Black 116
Spotted 117
Francolin, Coqui 43
Crested 42
Orange River 43

## G
Gallinule, Allen's 48
Go-away-bird, Grey 64
Goose, African Pygmy 28
Egyptian 27
Spur-winged 27
Goshawk, Dark Chanting 37
Gabar 38
Pale Chanting 37
Grebe, Little 25
Greenbul, Yellow-bellied 99
Greenshank, Common 57
Guineafowl, Helmeted 42
Gull, Grey-headed 59

## H
Hamerkop 16
Harrier, African Marsh 36
Harrier-Hawk, African 36
Hawk-Eagle, African 35
Helmetshrike, Retz's 88
White-crested 87
Heron, Black-crowned Night 17
Black-headed 19
Black 20
Goliath 19
Grey 18
Purple 19
Rufous-bellied 20
Squacco 18
Striated 18
White-backed Night 17
Hobby, Eurasian 42
Honeyguide, Greater 83
Hoopoe, African 74
Green Wood 74
Hornbill, African Grey 76
Bradfield's 76
Southern Ground 75
Southern Red-billed 75
Southern Yellow-billed 76

## I
Ibis, African Sacred 15
Glossy 15
Hadada 15
Indigobird, Village 129

## J
Jacana, African 49
Lesser 50

## K
Kestrel, Dickinson's 41
Greater 40
Rock 40
Kingfisher, Giant 78
Malachite 79
Pied 78
Striped 79
Woodland 79
Kite, Black-winged 39
Yellow-billed 36
Korhaan, Northern Black 47
Red-crested 46

## INDEX

**L**
Lapwing, African Wattled 52
　Blacksmith 52
　Crowned 52
　Long-toed 51
Lark, Dusky 94
　Eastern Clapper 95
　Fawn-coloured 95
　Monotonous 95
　Red-capped 96
　Rufous-naped 96
　Sabota 94
　Short-clawed 96
　Spike-heeled 94

**M**
Martin, Banded 99
　Brown-throated 100
　Sand 100
　Western House 100
Moorhen, Common 48
　Lesser 48
Mousebird, Red-faced 74
Myna, Common 111

**N**
Neddicky 106
Nightjar, Fiery-necked 72
　Rufous-cheeked 71
　Square-tailed 72

**O**
Openbill, African 22
Oriole, African Golden 90
　Black-headed 91
　Eurasian Golden 90
Ostrich, Common 45
Owl, African Scops 69
　Marsh 70
　Pel's Fishing 71
　Southern White-faced 70
　Western Barn 68
Owlet, African Barred 69
　Pearl-spotted 69
Oxpecker, Red-billed 114
　Yellow-billed 114

**P**
Painted-Snipe, Greater 54
Parrot, Meyer's 64
Pelican, Great White 14
　Pink-backed 14
Pigeon, African Green 64
　Speckled 61
Pipit, African 97
　Buffy 97
Plover, Caspian 53
　Chestnut-banded 53
　Common Ringed 53
　Kittlitz's 54
　Three-banded 54
Pochard, Southern 30
Pratincole, Collared 58
Prinia, Black-chested 107
　Tawny-flanked 107
Puffback, Black-backed 86
Pytilia, Green-winged 132

**Q**
Quail, Harlequin 44
Quelea, Red-billed 127

**R**
Robin, Kalahari Scrub 115
　White-browed Scrub 115
Robin-Chat, White-browed 116
Roller, Broad-billed 78
　European 77
　Lilac-breasted 77
　Purple 77
Ruff 55

**S**
Sandgrouse, Burchell's 61
　Double-banded 60
　Namaqua 60
Sandpiper, Common 56
　Curlew 55
　Marsh 57
　Wood 56
Scimitarbill, Common 75
Secretarybird 32
Shikra 38
Shoveler, Cape 28
Shrike, Crimson-breasted 87
　Lesser Grey 89
　Magpie 89
　Red-backed 90
　Southern White-crowned 88
Skimmer, African 59
Snipe, African 55

Sparrow, Cape 122
  Great 122
  House 123
  Southern Grey-headed 123
  Yellow-throated Bush 122
Sparrow-Lark, Chestnut-backed 93
  Grey-backed 93
Sparrow-Weaver, White-browed 124
Sparrowhawk, Little 39
  Ovambo 38
Spoonbill, African 14
Spurfowl, Natal 44
  Red-billed 43
  Swainson's 44
Starling, Burchell's 113
  Cape 112
  Greater Blue-eared 112
  Meves's 112
  Red-winged 113
  Violet-backed 113
  Wattled 111
Stilt, Black-winged 51
Stint, Little 56
Stonechat, African 118
Stork, Abdim's 23
  African Woolly-necked 24
  Marabou 22
  Saddle–billed 24
  White 23
  Yellow-billed 23
Sunbird, Amethyst 120
  Collared 120
  Dusky 121
  Marico 121
  Scarlet-chested 120
  White-bellied 121
Swallow, Barn 101
  Greater Striped 102
  Lesser Striped 102
  Pearl-breasted 101
  Red-breasted 102
  Wire-tailed 101
Swamphen, African 47
Swift, African Palm 72
  Common 73
  Little 73
  White-rumped 73

T

Tchagra, Black-crowned 85
  Brown-crowned 86
Teal, Blue-billed 28
  Cape 29
  Red-billed 29
Tern, Whiskered 59
  White-winged 60
Thick-knee, Spotted 50
  Water 50
Thrush, Groundscraper 114
  Kurrichane 115
Tit, Ashy 92
  Cape Penduline 93
  Southern Black 92

V

Vulture, Cape 31
  Hooded 30
  Lappet-faced 31
  White-backed 31
  White-headed 32

W

Wagtail, African Pied 98
  Cape 97
Warbler, Chestnut-vented 109
  Common Reed 104
  Icterine 104
  Lesser Swamp 103
  Little Rush 103
  Rufous-eared 107
  Willow 104
Waxbill, Black-faced 130
  Blue 131
  Common 130
  Violet-eared 131
Weaver, Holub's Golden 125
  Lesser Masked 125
  Red-billed Buffalo 123
  Red-headed 126
  Scaly-feathered 125
  Sociable 124
  Southern Masked 126
  Thick-billed 124
  Village 126
Wheatear, Capped 119
White-eye, Southern Yellow 110
Whydah, Long-tailed Paradise 129
  Pin-tailed 128
  Shaft-tailed 128
Widowbird, Fan-tailed 128
Woodpecker, Bearded 84
  Bennett's 83
  Cardinal 84
  Golden-tailed 83
Wren-Warbler, Barred 108